THE EAST KENT RAILWAY
THE LINE THAT RAN TO NOWHERE

Dedication

In memory of Ivor Gotheridge, an eccentric railway enthusiast and friend, who loved the East Kent Railway and travelled on it during his periodic holidays in Dover, sampling the delights of a truly British light railway.

THE EAST KENT RAILWAY
THE LINE THAT RAN TO NOWHERE

JOHN SCOTT-MORGAN

AN IMPRINT OF PEN & SWORD BOOKS LTD.
YORKSHIRE – PHILADELPHIA

First published in Great Britain in 2021 by
Pen and Sword Transport
An imprint of
Pen & Sword Books Ltd
Yorkshire - Philadelphia

Copyright © John Scott-Morgan, 2021

ISBN 978 1 52672 685 8

The right of John Scott-Morgan to be identified as Author of this work has been asserted by him in accordance with the Copyright, Designs and Patents Act 1988.

A CIP catalogue record for this book is available from the British Library.

All rights reserved. No part of this book may be reproduced or transmitted in any form or by any means, electronic or mechanical including photocopying, recording or by any information storage and retrieval system, without permission from the Publisher in writing.

Typeset by SJmagic DESIGN SERVICES, India.
Printed and bound in India by Replika Press Pvt. Ltd.

Pen & Sword Books Ltd incorporates the Imprints of Pen & Sword Books Archaeology, Atlas, Aviation, Battleground, Discovery, Family History, History, Maritime, Military, Naval, Politics, Railways, Select, Transport, True Crime, Fiction, Frontline Books, Leo Cooper, Praetorian Press, Seaforth Publishing, Wharncliffe and White Owl.

For a complete list of Pen & Sword titles please contact

PEN & SWORD BOOKS LIMITED
47 Church Street, Barnsley, South Yorkshire, S70 2AS, England
E-mail: enquiries@pen-and-sword.co.uk
Website: www.pen-and-sword.co.uk

or

PEN AND SWORD BOOKS
1950 Lawrence Rd, Havertown, PA 19083, USA
E-mail: Uspen-and-sword@casematepublishers.com
Website: www.penandswordbooks.com

Contents

Acknowledgements	6
Bibliography	7
Introduction	8
So Much Promise and So Little Reward (The Kent Coalfield)	10
The East Kent Railway (A Journey on the Road to Canterbury)	12
The East Kent Railway (A Brief History)	14
The East Kent Railway: The Preservation Years by Graeme Gleaves	20
The Main Line – Shepherdswell to Wingham Canterbury Road	24
The Richborough Port Branch	86
The Last Day of Passenger Traffic	94
The British Railways Period	96
The Weed Killing Train	110
Tilmanstone and Guilford Collieries	114
The Locomotive Fleet	120
Locomotives on Loan to the East Kent Railway	161
The Carriage Stock	165
The Wagon Fleet	179
Shepherdswell Shed and Works	188
Cover Pictures	194
The Preserved Line	196

Acknowledgements

I would like to thank the following people for their kind assistance during the writing of this volume, I would especially like to thank the late Richard Casserley who very kindly gave me permission to use his pictures from the H.C. Casserley collection, there are also pictures from the late Rev A.W. Mace, Ivor Gotheridge, J.W. Sparrow, S.W. Baker, Dennis Cullum, R.F. Roberts via Stephenson Locomotive Society, P.J. Garland, E.A. Woollard, Derek Cross via David Cross, A.W. Croughton, Ron Jarvis, G.S. Lloyd, C.T. Hamilton-Ellis, F. Butterfield and Tom Middlemass.

I would also like to thank the following for use of pictures, R.S. Carpenter, J.H. Aston, J.C.V. Mitchell, R.C. Stumpf, G. Gleeves and the LCGB Ken Nunn Collection.

I have made every effort to contact the copyright holders of pictures used in this book, however if I have left anyone out, I apologise and please contact me through the publisher.

Bibliography

Clapper, C.H. and Dalston, H.F.G., 'East Kent Light Railway', *Railway Magazine* March 1937.

Kidner, R.W., *Standard Gauge Light Railways*, Oakwood Press 1973.

Lawson Finch, M. and Garratt, S.R., *The East Kent Railway Volumes 1 & 2,* Oakwood Press, both 2003.

Mitchell, Vic and Smith, Keith, *The East Kent Light Railway*, Middleton Press 1989.

Introduction

A long time ago, in the early 1980s, I went by car with my friend Ivor Gotheridge on a New Year's Day car journey. It was very cold and there was snow on the ground, as we ventured further and further into East Kent. After an hour and a half we reached our destination, Tilmanstone Colliery in the East Kent coalfield, which was about to cease production and close.

We passed the colliery and continued along a route not far from the long abandoned road bed of the East Kent Railway, until we reached Eastry, which had been the junction for the lines to Canterbury Road and the branch to Richborough Port, past the abutments of the long abandoned over bridge, from where we made our way to the site of Canterbury Road station, which was by then just a tump of earth, with a shallow cutting running from it.

We got out of the car and Ivor explained to me the former track layout and how Dick Haffrey, the station agent, had a lonely vigil each day waiting for the few trains that operated that part of the line.

We then headed out towards Richborough Port and arrived at the site of the former bridge that had once crossed the SE&CR coastal main line near Richborough, the abandoned bridge abutments standing sentinel each side of the railway, looking gaunt and ghostly in the late afternoon winter sun shine.

We retraced our journey along the line, back to Eastry and then on to the site of Guilford Colliery, which had been largely constructed but never opened, some of its brick buildings still standing in the remains of the colliery yard, after which we drove to Elvington, where we found the remains of the brick platform, in a shallow cutting overgrown by brambles.

On the way back to Shepherdswell, Ivor stopped the car, so I could walk through Golgotha tunnel, which was constructed for two tracks, but only ever had a single line through it. As I walked through the tunnel, torch in hand, I could see the blocks of uncut chalk that had not been excavated from the second line, through the tunnel.

I was met at the other side by Ivor and we made our way to Shepherdswell to see the remains of the East Kent Railway station and the site of the former locomotive shed.

It was a bleak site, with two sidings occupying the remains of the former platform and the flat expanse of the area that had once been the locomotive shed and works.

This was my first visit to the East Kent Railway, a line that had opened just before the First World War with such great expectations and had become something of a great disappointment to its promoters and those who financed the venture. Over the next few years, I made other journeys to the line, often meeting former employees of the railway and gleaning interesting information and anecdotes, about this eccentric backwater that once seemingly had so much promise.

So Much Promise and So Little Reward (The Kent Coalfield)

The ill-fated attempt to construct a Channel Tunnel in the 1880s–1890s had one major benefit, the discovery of coal in Kent. Despite the first Channel Tunnel project being abandoned in the late 1890s, the prospect of being able to exploit a sizable new coalfield interested and excited investors looking to make money out of this unexpected bonus. Even so, despite the discovery of coal in the Dover, Folkestone area it took some years to organise any meaningful attempt to exploit it. Test borings were carried out in the last decade of the nineteenth century, with mixed results. However, exploration of a more serious nature started to take place in the first decade of the twentieth century, resulting in a number of collieries opening up and producing sizable quantities of coal.

The main collieries were at Tilmanstone, Chislet, Snowdown and Betteshanger; other workings were attempted but were found to be either uneconomic or difficult to work for geological reasons, so were soon abandoned. There was also a colliery near Dover which was in production from 1896 to 1915, though this pit closed due to poor quality coal and continual severe flooding.

Further collieries were almost completed at Wingham and Stonehall south of Shepherdswell, which were under construction just before the outbreak of the First World War; however, as a result of the war and other factors, the project to complete the pits were mothballed and never resumed after the war.

The East Kent coal was found to be not of the same quality as that of the Yorkshire, Nottinghamshire, or south Wales coal fields and this often resulted in the East Kent product being mixed with coal from other coal fields for use in transport or industry.

Among the original investors in the East Kent Coalfield were a number of foreign companies based in parts of Europe, including France, Germany and at least one company which was registered in St Petersburg in Tsarist Russia.

The East Kent Railway was originally meant to serve four collieries, that of Tilmanstone, which successfully opened in 1912; Guilford abandoned before opening in 1920; Hammill, abandoned before opening in 1914; and Wingham, abandoned in 1914.

A French Company purchased Guilford and Stonehall collieries in 1919, but soon found that the serious flooding problems that dogged the original owners also made things impossible for them, which led to the abandonment of both projects in 1921. The buildings at Hammill Colliery were converted into a brick works, which successfully operated for many years, providing traffic to the light railway.

The four successful collieries in Kent functioned from the First World War through to the late 1980s, when, one by one, each of them finally closed, Chislet being the first in 1969, followed by Tilmanstone and Snowdown in 1987, with Betteshanger being the last to close in 1989.

Quite apart from the quality of the coal from the Kent coalfield, the area suffered from industrial problems which often made operational matters difficult. The coal industry in Kent almost lasted for a century, the high hopes of the 1880s when the new coalfield was discovered gradually turned to disappointment during the early twentieth century, when it was discovered that things were not as good as first envisaged, finally ending after the miners' strike in the mid-1980s, after which the last mines finally closed.

The East Kent Railway
(A Journey on the Road to Canterbury)

There are those who say that it is sometimes better to travel hopefully than arrive; this statement would certainly be true, where the East Kent Railway was concerned, a light railway that was promoted to serve the newly-developing Kent coalfield, which was meant to create wealth and prosperity for its investors and many jobs in the coastal area near Dover and Folkestone.

In truth, although a number of collieries were opened and produced coal, the majority of the mines envisaged for the area, were never constructed or operational. The East Kent Railway was to be a pivotal part in the development of this coalfield, providing the transport for the minerals out of the area, both via the South Eastern & Chatham Railway at Shepherdswell and after the First World War, through the port of Richborough, from where coal would be exported to Europe and elsewhere.

There were many factors that prevented the original plans from coming to fruition, partly economic and partly due to geology, in that, although many areas were tested and bore holes were drilled into the ground, it was found that some parts of the landscape where coal was thought to exist had little or no sizable yield of the mineral. There were also projected collieries where shafts were dug and due to serious flooding the scheme put on ice, or abandoned for lack of capital or for geological problems.

On the route of the East Kent Railway, this was certainly the situation at three projected colliery sites, at Guilford near Tilmanstone, where the colliery buildings were constructed and shafts dug, but coal production never started; at Hammill, which later became a brick works; and at Wingham, where the surface buildings were constructed but no coal production took place. The only colliery to successfully open and produce good quantities of coal was Tilmanstone, opened in 1912.

Sir Edward Watkin, chairman of the South Eastern Railway, had originally been involved in test borings near Dover in the early 1880s; however, although coal was discovered in thin seams in the Dover area, it was felt that the South Eastern Railway did not possess the powers to take the project any further and it was left in the hands of other parties to progress the project.

There was clearly a need to provide a good railway connection, if the various projects were to succeed and in the last years of peace before the First World War, it was decided to promote and construct a series of light railways to connect and transport coal from the envisaged pits, the engineer in charge of the project being Holman Fred Stephens, who had already proved himself by successfully opening a number of light railways using the Light Railways Act 1896.

Holman Fred Stephens was often consulted by parties wishing to construct new or reinstate old lines as light railways, in having an established engineering practice based at Salford Terrace Tonbridge Kent. His able assistant was William H. Austin, who Stephens first met during the construction of the Cranbrook and Paddock Wood Railway in the early 1890s. Stephens was a rather colourful character in the professional railway world, with unusual and sometimes quite progressive ideas to promote light railway schemes.

One could say that as far as the nineteenth and early twentieth centuries are concerned, the light railway age, which began in the late 1890s was the last stage in the development of the traditional railway.

The East Kent Railway
(A Brief History)

The East Kent Railway was probably one of the most disappointing light railway projects ever undertaken by railway investors in the early twentieth century. The light railway was meant to open up the Kent coalfield et seq. and make large profits for its shareholders, who had high hopes of both making money from the collieries and from the railway.

The first section of line connected exchange sidings at Shepherdswell, on the Canterbury Dover line of the London Chatham & Dover Railway, later South Eastern & Chatham Railway, with the line to Tilmanstone colliery, opened in December 1911, for freight traffic. This first section of line was constructed on a temporary formation, which was shortly after lifted, when the permanent line was constructed, through a tunnel through Golgotha Hill.

In October 1912, the line had been extended to Eastry, with a branch to Guilford Colliery, which was under construction at the time. By December, the line had reached Hammill and Wingham running northwards from Eastry and construction of collieries at both points was well under way. Tilmanstone colliery went into production in 1914, which gave the light railway some ongoing revenue, however partly due to the outbreak of the First World War and problems raising the capital for both the collieries and the light railway, progress was slow during and after the war period.

The line was not opened to passenger traffic until 16 October 1916, on the section between Shepherdswell and Wingham Colliery, being extended to Wingham Town in 1920.

During the war, a large port had been constructed at Richborough to transport military equipment and heavy supplies to France, using train ferries. It was hoped that the East Kent Railway would provide a connection with this port and benefit from large tonnages of coal being exported from there.

However, despite the construction of an extension from Eastry to Richborough Port and halts being established and passenger services opening along this line, which opened as far as Sandwich Road in 1925, further passenger services to Richborough Port never materialised, partly due to the poor construction of the bridges at the Richborough end of

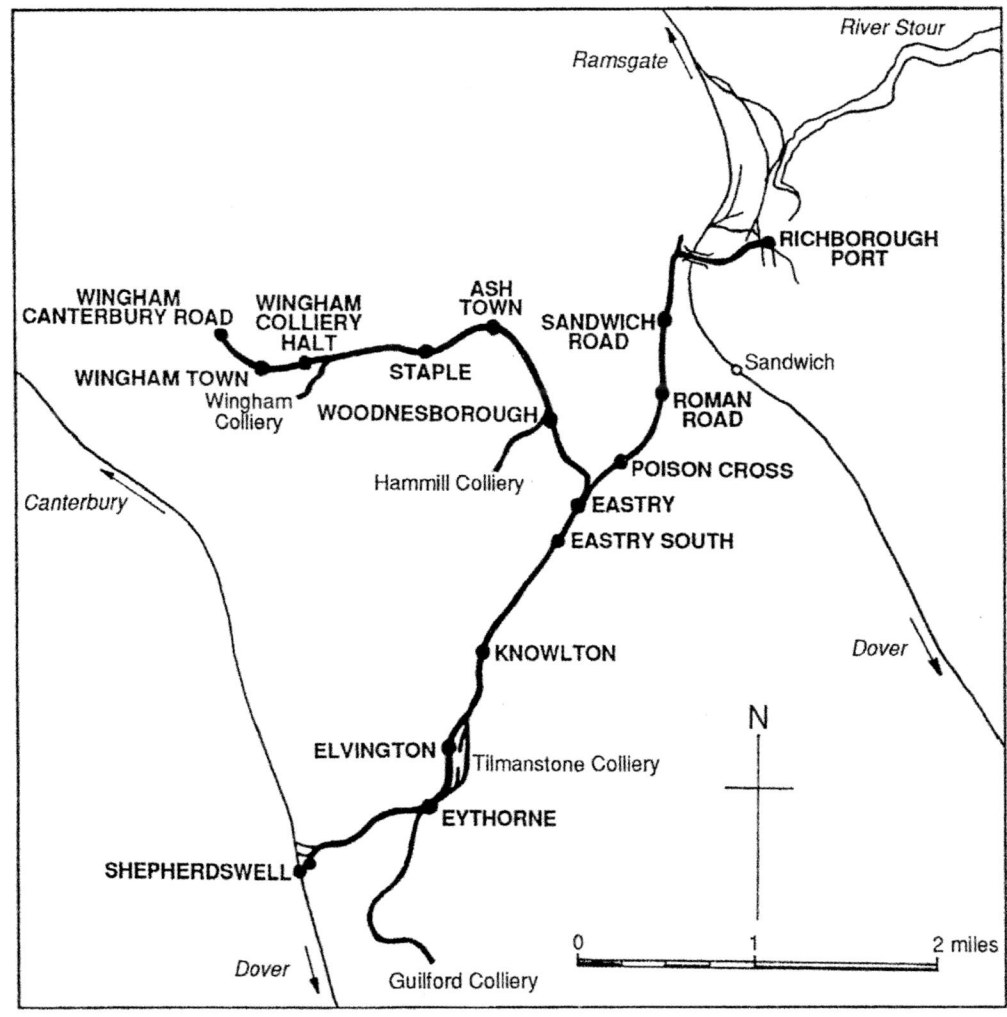

the branch, which crossed the river Stour and the Southern Railway's main line from Sandwich to Minster Junction.

The other reason for the failure of the company to operate trains along this stretch of the system was that the company was not on good terms with the owners of Richborough Port, Pearson & Dorman Long, colliery owners and, in the North of England, steel manufacturers. Pearson & Dorman Long had intended to construct a steel works near Richborough Port and set up a coal export operation from the port; however, this project was later cancelled. They wanted nothing to do with this poorly financed, rickety railway, which snaked its way across east Kent, serving collieries that had been half constructed and then abandoned.

The East Kent Railway withdrew passenger services after only three years from the Richborough Branch, this taking place on 31 October 1928, when the last passenger service ran from Sandwich Road. After the passenger service ceased along the Richborough branch, only the occasional freight train operated, on a when-required basis.

The main line from Shepherdswell to Wingham Canterbury Road also had a basic passenger service of two trains a day, often a mixed formation of freight wagons and a single carriage. The mainstay of traffic on the line lay in the output from Tilmanstone Colliery, the brick works at Hammill and some agricultural traffic, often of a seasonal nature. The light railway did make enough revenue for the Southern Railway to feel optimistic about its future, as the Southern invested in the East Kent Railway in the inter-war period and had a sizable interest of £300,000 in the company. During the early years of the venture, the company had been optimistic, projecting some forty light railway orders for future extensions to the system of lines. However, by the inter-war period, this was a thing of the past and the light railway settled down to a kind of pastoral slumber, apart from the section between Tilmanstone Colliery and the exchange sidings at Shepherdswell, where there was always some activity.

The sight of an elderly 0 class 0-6-0 tender goods coated in a layer of grime, hauling a string of various wagons and a weather beaten six wheeler carriage, across fields of wheat or cabbages must have been an amazing sight to behold.

Often the carriage had one passenger, or two if you were lucky, stopping at the way side halts and basic stations with primitive buildings that looked for all the world like garden sheds. The station agents at these way side places had a lonely existence, with only two trains a day and little to do between them.

In the winter, it must have been an eerie journey from Wingham Canterbury Road to Shepherdswell, with the dim lights of the four or six wheeled carriage and the dark fields either side of the train, as it ran through the inky darkness to the next station with its dim oil lamps illuminating the bleak platform. On winter nights like that, especially after a snow storm, the crew of the old 01 class locomotive with its small open inadequate cab, would huddle near the fire, only having the sound of the locomotive's exhaust beat for company.

At Shepherdswell, the locomotive would detach from its single carriage and run into the shed, where the crew would dispose of it, while the train guard would use the hand brake to gravitate the train into the station platform, after which the guard would secure the train, lock the carriage doors and take the day's takings in a cloth bag to the small office in the timber station building, putting it in the office drawer in the desk and locking it, before locking the door and making tracks for home.

In the summer, the gypsy train would gently haul its load of wagons and a single passenger carriage through fields of corn or vegetables towards Wingham Canterbury Road station, where again gravity shunting would take place, this time with the locomotive running forward of a set of points near the level crossing that led to the platform in the shallow cutting. The rolling stock would then gravitate into the siding, which often had a hay stack next to it, the grass being cut from the banks each side of the line by the permanent way gang.

Next, the passengers would be ushered down from the train by the guard, who used a porter's barrow or a ladder from the brake vehicle to decant the few passengers, to the ground.

The company was always trying to save money, so this was a way of not having to construct a more elaborate arrangement involving a run around loop, at the station.

Like all the lines operated by Colonel Stephens, there were interesting incidents, like the time a portly farmer appeared by the side of the line with baskets of farm produce. Trying to stop the slow running train by putting his hand out, as if it were a bus, the train crew ran their train by ignoring the farmer to their peril, for when they returned a few hours later, the now angry portly farmer, bombarded the cab of the locomotive with rotten tomatoes and apples.

Stories are told of the time a train crew were playing a game of darts in a local pub at Wingham and held the train up until one of them won the darts game, to see who paid for the drinks, the problem being a local magistrate was on the train, waiting for it to leave, so he could attend the local assizes that morning. He walked down to the pub and asked the train crew when the train was likely to depart, to which the locomotive driver said, 'Hang on guv, we have to see who wins the game, to see who pays for the beer.' They were reported to Colonel Stephens, who was not very happy with them.

Perhaps one of the most bizarre stories involved the Royal Engineers, who operated Ex-Great Western Dean Goods locomotives and rail mounted guns along the line in the early years of the Second World War. The Royal Engineers and the army were there as part of the South Coast defences, after the fall of France in the spring and summer of 1940. An Engineers locomotive crew decided to bull up their dull painted Dean Goods and not only polish it but shine the brass and copper fittings on the locomotive. The smart looking, black painted Dean Goods was out with a rail mounted gun on the little-used Richborough Port branch, when the bored locomotive crew decided to detach the locomotive from its gun and run forward to see how far they could go towards Richborough Port. The locomotive and its crew worked their way along the long abandoned and overgrown line, until they reached the rickety bridge over the Southern Railway's Main Line near Sandwich, where they stopped in the centre of the long-abandoned bridge, which had not been maintained for some twenty years.

Presently, a semi-fast train headed by a former SE&CR 4-4-0 tender locomotive appeared, with the Southern crew waving frantically to the engineers' locomotive crew. The Sappers on the Dean Goods footplate thought that this was fun and waved back, after which the Southern train went out of sight heading towards Minster Junction. Shortly after the incident, the two engineers found themselves on a charge and in front of their commanding officer, who demanded an explanation as the bridge they were standing on could have collapsed at any moment. He was also not happy with the bulled up Dean Goods, which could have attracted attention from the Luftwaffe and ordered it to be painted dull black again.

During the war years, the line became more profitable, with extra traffic on the main line to Wingham Canterbury Road, where there was now more agricultural traffic and also the line benefited from the transportation of military stores and ammunition to Staple, where there was an RAF station nearby. After the war in Europe came to an end in May 1945, things started to slow down and by the late 1940s, the line had lost a great deal of its traffic, apart from the colliery traffic from Tilmanstone.

Sometime before nationalisation in January 1948, there was talk of cutting back services to Tilmanstone Colliery and withdrawing the passenger service. Plans existed for the recently acquired Ex-L&SWR corridor bogie brake carriages to be transferred to the Kent & East Sussex Railway, if the passenger service ceased.

On 1 January 1948, the East Kent Railway became officially nationalised; however, because so many new arrangements had to be put in place for the main line companies, the original company continued to run things until the May of that year, from Salford Terrace in Tonbridge Kent. W.H. Austen, who had taken over management of the group of light railways, after the death of Colonel Stephens in October 1931, stayed in control for the first five months of state control, before retiring.

Quite understandably, the newly formed British Railways were not that impressed with their new acquisition, having the derelict carriage and wagon stock broken up at Shepherdswell, soon after taking control and deciding equally quickly to close the line to all passenger traffic from 30 October 1948, with freight services continuing for a time on the whole of the main line. However, this arrangement gradually changed as the freight service was cut back, starting with the section from Wingham Canterbury Road to Eastry on 25 July 1950 and Eythorne to Eastry on 1 July 1951, the Richborough Port branch had closed from Eastry to Richborough Port on 27 October 1949.

After the closures of the main line and Richborough Port branch, only the section from the exchange sidings at Shepherdswell to Tilmanstone Colliery remained in use, the shed at Shepherdswell having closed after passenger services ceased in 1948, after which locomotives were supplied by Dover locomotive shed.

The locomotives inherited by British Railways, were at least on paper given new numbers in the Southern Region numbering system, but apart from East Kent Railway 01 class No. 2, formally No. 100, which became 31383, all the other locomotives that survived in 1948, Nos. 4, Victory class, 6, 01 highbred, 7, Ex-L&SWR E0127, together with 01 class 1371, were never renumbered and were withdrawn soon after nationalisation.

After the coal industry was nationalised in 1947, the newly formed National Coal Board took over shunting the colliery sidings at Tilmanstone, using an 0-4-0 Hunslet diesel mechanical shunter, as a result of which, the link with the former East Kent Railway providing this service ended.

In 1930, Tilmanstone Colliery constructed a five mile long aerial rope way, connecting the colliery with Dover harbour; the coal was deposited into a 5,000 ton capacity bunker for onward shipment abroad. The aerial ropeway cost £97,000 and was designed to remove the monopoly the East Kent Railway had on the colliery.

The 01 class 0-6-0 tender goods locomotives became the mainstay of the line throughout the 1950s and into the early 1960s, until 1961 when the last member of the class, 31065, was withdrawn and which is now preserved on the Bluebell Railway in East Sussex, along with the Adams Radial Tank No. 5.

After Kent coast electrification, steam was eliminated from Kent, except Ashford Works which had an allocation of departmental locomotives, three C class 0-6-0 tender goods locomotives and two USA tanks, cascaded from Southampton Docks, for shunting the wagon works.

There was for a time, until 1964, steam operations on the Tonbridge to Reading line, with a small number of steam locomotives allocated to Tonbridge and Redhill sheds, but in truth, main line steam traction finished in Kent in 1962.

On the East Kent Railway, the end of steam traction meant the allocation of class 08 and later 09 class, 350 H P diesel mechanical 0-6-0 shunters, with occasional workings of class 73 electro diesel Bo-Bo locomotives, hauling the coal wagons from Tilmanstone Colliery to the exchange sidings at Shepherdswell and shunting the storage sidings.

The final end of what was left of the light railway, came after the miners' strike was declared in 1984, when trains of coal from Tilmanstone Colliery ceased on 1 March, never to be resumed.

The light railway would have been lifted and demolished in normal circumstances after a final decision had been made over its future, however fate decreed otherwise, as a preservation society was formed to save the line from Tilmanstone Colliery to the former East Kent Railway station at Shepherdswell. The East Kent Railway Preservation Society had managed to obtain a lease on the line from Tilmanstone to Shepherdswell by 1990, with a plan to set up a museum and restore the line for passenger operation.

To date, the preservation society has successfully restored the line from Shepherdswell to Eythorne, with plans to restore and operate over the line towards the former Guilford Colliery.

The former colliery site at Tilmanstone is used by the society for rolling stock storage and restoration of locomotives.

So almost 110 years after the first stage of the East Kent Railway opened, there is still a Colonel Stephens light railway, in East Kent and long may it flourish.

The East Kent Railway
The Preservation Years
by Graeme Gleaves

Following the closure of the line by British Rail and with no prospect for any further rail traffic for the route or the East Kent Light Railway station site at Shepherdswell, a group of enthusiasts had the idea of acquiring the remaining section of the EKLR and opening it as a heritage railway. Kent was not short of tourist lines at this time. The Kent and East Sussex, Sittingbourne and Kemsley and the Romney Hythe and Dymchurch lines were all doing good business but it was felt there was an opportunity for a standard gauge line in the east of the county and given the availability of the route wheels were put in motion during 1985.

The driving force behind the venture was the mining engineer Dr Robert Kinghorn who, along with his good friend and fellow mining engineer Dr Alfred Minter, organised an initial meeting for those interest in founding such a project. Word of mouth and well placed editorials in various publications got the message out and the meeting was convened at Biggin Hall in Dover during November 1985. In the event, Dr Kinghorn was unable to attend but he sent Ivor Gotheridge in his place, who spoke enthusiastically to the well-attended event and it was here that the East Kent Railway Society was formed with Dr Minter as its initial Chairman and a committee put together from willing volunteers. Those wishing to join the society queued up at the end of the meeting to pay their subs and from there the ball was well and truly rolling.

Meetings were held with the British Rail Property Board over the next few months to negotiate not only the purchase of the trackbed but to arrange access to it so work on clearance could commence and thus the job of creating a heritage railway could begin. The society became a registered charity during 1987 and, with the inevitable early personnel changes continued to make progress in acquiring the site. A limited company, The East Kent Light Railway Ltd, was formed and it was this which took on the role of land purchase and also purchasing the remaining trackwork that was under threat of being lifted and sold for scrap; the society had until that point been leasing it. The Shepherdswell site was fenced and work started to construct the station there, sympathetically to the original Colonel Stephens style.

The first rolling stock began to arrive in 1990. April saw a Fowler, on loan from British Coal, become the first loco on site, followed in November by an English Electric 0-6-0 diesel that had been purchased privately by a group of EKLR members from British Coal. The loco had been stored at Stonar until the site could accept it. Ownership of the loco was transferred to the EKLR Ltd and in due course, the loco was given the name *Richborough Castle* in keeping with the heritage of the route it was to operate. Over the next few years, further wagons, coaches and some locos arrived at the site; a notable example was the unique Leyland experimental coach, which was an attempt to build a new style of hauled carriage for British Rail using a Leyland body but the prototype was as far as the project got. Steam locos arrived in the form of a rare 0-6-0 'Minnie' built by Fox Walker in 1878. Another was an 0-6-0 saddle tank named *St Dunstan* that was built by Avonside in 1927 and worked at Snowdown Colliery. Neither loco was in operational condition and only *St Dunstan* remains at the railway to this day, having been cosmetically restored for display with future operational restoration a long term project. The first viable passenger stock was a Mk. 1 suburban compartment coach and motive power in the form of an 08 (08108) diesel shunting loco, privately purchased from British Rail. The guard's brake at one end of the carriage had a lookout cut into it so it could act in a push-pull capacity with the 08 and it was this formation that carried the first passengers from the station built at Shepherdswell as far as the Eythorne Road level crossing less than a third of a mile away. The railway had obtained its light railway order to permit running across public highways on 1 September 1993 but the infrastructure was still not in place yet to run a passenger service to Eythorne itself.

The day of the first public runs to Eythorne was 24 June 1995, less than ten years after the idea of starting the railway was mooted. Locomotives and rolling stock had come and gone and the first choice passenger stock by this time was a pair of two-car diesel mechanical units, a type not normally associated with the area but, given the large numbers that were available for preservation and the low running costs, these were a good choice. Two sets were obtained, a class 108 in Network SouthEast livery, the other a class 107 that had been in service in Scotland and presented the highly unusual sight of a train painted in the Strathclyde Passenger Transport Executive livery of orange and black in the Kent countryside. The new stations at both Shepherdswell and Eythorne were built with platforms only just long enough to accommodate one two coach train, so the units were not run together. In the event, it was the 108 that proved more reliable and this saw more use during the early years when the railway was establishing itself.

The EKLR Ltd had obtained both the track and trackbed for the surviving line; this included the section beyond

Eythorne towards Tilmanstone Colliery where the line ended at Wigmore Lane, a missing bridge preventing any further progress. From the outset, the section of line beyond Eythorne was not considered to be part of the passenger operations and has only been used to store wagons and other stock. The level crossing at Eythorne is maintained but very rarely used. Eythorne has seen many changes since the railway opened. The platform was constructed on almost the exact site of the original and was brick faced. It was just long enough to accommodate a two car DMU and was extended by another coach length back towards Shepherdswell with a wooden plank deck and timber supports. There is a station waiting shelter built by the EKLR volunteers and the signal box from Selling was erected here at the level crossing end of the station platform. It is not functioning as a working box but has been restored and now houses artefacts and photos on the history of the line. The station car park houses a scaled replica of pit winding gear in keeping with the heritage of the line and its association with the Kent coal fields. Two sidings are located at the rear of the station controlled by a ground frame mounted in a cabin at the point where the Guilford colliery branch used to diverge. The sidings host a few wagons but most significantly the ex-Southern Railway bogie elephant van which is fitted out as a working cafeteria and opens five days a week during most of the year.

   Shepherdswell has a single platform station with a ticket office constructed in the style of Colonel Stephens. The site also houses the signal box from Barham, which, like the box located at Eythorne, is restored and used as a museum building. The site has seen massive development since the early years of operations, helped in part by a £50,000 grant from the National Lottery. A small miniature railway was installed by a local model engineering group in the early years but this has been enhanced and a seven and a quarter inch gauge miniature railway now runs in the station's woodland walk area and extends for over a quarter of a mile. There is a large cafe in a permanent building that is open five days a week and a local model railway group has set up an extensive display inside an ex-LMS carriage that is permanently parked on a spur adjacent to the station and has accessible steps and a ramp.

   Over the years, locomotives and rolling stock continued to change. The 107 and 108 DMUs moved on and a Regional Railways Metro Cammel built class 101 two car DMU which gave good service for a few years until it too moved on. The railway acquired a two car class 205 'thumper' DEMU which was more in keeping with its geographic location and this continues to see use on passenger services on the line. Various industrial diesel shunters have been based there and the current fleet includes some ex-MOD 4wd Vanguard diesel hydraulic locos fitted with air train brakes. The class 08 and 09s were frequent visitors to the line in the latter years of British Rail operation and both classes have been represented during the preservation years. The original class 08 moved on to the Kent and East Sussex railway whilst a class 09 was based there and operated for a number of years before moving to the Lavender Line in Sussex. Four class 08s are currently operational at the EKLR and see frequent use on passenger operations. These are the only ex-main line diesel classes to have worked the line in preservation, although that may change in the near future.

Steam is the main draw for any heritage railway and the EKLR has never had an operational loco of its own so had to rely on hiring ones in. The first came in the shape of Bagnall 0-6-0 *Brookfield*, which visited for the 1996 August bank holiday. The following year, Barclay 0-4-0 *Spitfire* visited for Easter and then RSH 0-4-0 *AJAX* from Chatham Dockyard spent several months during the summer and autumn operating on the line. In 2019, the railway took a financial gamble and hired in Peckett 0-4-0 *Achilles* for the summer season. The gamble paid off and the loco will be returning to the line to operate again in 2020.

One area the East Kent Railway has been notably progressive in is the representation of preserved electric stock. The railway has hosted far more examples of this than any other heritage line in the 'Southern Electric' area. Examples of EPB, CEP, VEP, COR and motor luggage vans have resided there over the years. The current stock list includes a complete 4-VOP unit, two coaches of a 4-COR, one of which is regularly used as hauled stock, the unique 457 driving motor car which is parked in the bay at Eythorne and a driving trailer composite from a Ramsgate based 4-VEP unit that was acquired from the National Railway Museum and refurbished by the East Kent to blue and grey livery so that it is regularly used in passenger trains.

A drive by the management of the line to improve the visitor experience saw new ventures such as catering trains, cream teas and more running days as well as the return of steam to the line. All of this has paid dividends, with visitor numbers that were below 1,000 in 2014 reaching 10,000 in 2019. Not surprisingly, there are new projects in the pipeline. February 2020 saw the arrival of a class 142 Pacer DMU to begin regular operations; a class that has never operated anywhere in Kent before and will certainly be a novel experience. A second example is due to arrive some time during the year to join it. New sidings are being laid to accommodate rolling stock for the railway and its chosen partners over the next twelve to eighteen months. Perhaps the most exciting plan involves the re-instatement of half a mile of the former Guilford Colliery branch from Eythorne; this will make this station an interchange once more. The railway that began as a pipe dream over 35 years ago has gone through tough times but appears to be going from strength to strength.

The Main Line – Shepherdswell to Wingham Canterbury Road

A large group of railway navvies pose for a photograph, during the construction of the first section of the East Kent Railway, c1911.
(Author's Collection)

A shareholders' special train headed by Fox Walker constructed saddle tank No. 1, on 27 November 1912. The carriage behind the locomotive is a former Kent & East Sussex bogie brake vehicle, which was transferred to the East Kent Railway, to provide the line's first passenger vehicle. This carriage was originally Kent & East Sussex Railway No. 17, being constructed by R.Y. Pickering in May 1905 and numbered 1, on the East Kent Railway, withdrawn by British Railways in 1948. *(Ivor Gotheridge Collection)*

The approach path to the platform at Shepherdswell East Kent Railway station in August 1937, showing the rather basic station building and two six-wheeled carriages, No. 5, an ex-L&SWR brake third and ex-Midland Railway composite No. 4, standing in the platform. The carriage in the background far left is carriage No. 7, an ex-LC&DR four compartment all third, obtained from the SE&CR in 1920, broken up in 1947 or 1948. *(R.S. Carpenter Collection)*

On the same day, a view from the other end of the platform, looking towards the buffer stops, showing the two six-wheel carriages and a line of interesting open wagons including three obtained from the SE&CR and a former North London Railway, four-wheeled passenger brake van No. 2. This was one of two purchased from William Jones of London in 1904, for the Kent & East Sussex Railway, being later transferred to the East Kent Railway, August 1937. *(R.S. Carpenter Collection)*

The scene a year later, looking towards the buffer stops on Saturday, 24 September 1938, showing the siding with assorted freight wagons and freight stock waiting in the platform. There was no run round loop at this location, which meant that trains had to be marshalled in the approach yard and shunted down to the passenger platform. In the distance can be seen the station building and the corrugated iron circular storage hut on the far left. *(R.F. Roberts, Stephenson Locomotive Society)*

Shepherdswell Station from the bank above the platform, showing the two sidings crammed full of rolling stock on 25 September 1948. Hybrid 01 class 0-6-0 tender goods No. 6, is about to back down with the next train to Canterbury Road, only a month before closure to passengers. *(J.H. Aston)*

A close-up of No. 6 and its train of a single Ex-L&SWR bogie corridor carriage No. 5, constructed in 1911 and obtained from the Southern Railway in July 1946, one of two such vehicles costing £75 each, 25 September 1948. *(J.H. Aston)*

A view from the base of the incline section, connecting the exchange sidings on the main line with the light railway, c1937, showing the track layout at the station and the ramshackle arrangement of sleepers and rail. Note the arrangement of the sleepers on the point, far right of the picture. *(Ivor Gotheridge Collection)*

Hybrid 01 class 0-6-0 tender goods No. 6 departs Shepherdswell with a mixed train service to Canterbury Road in the summer of 1947.
(Author's Collection)

East Kent Railway O1 class No. 100 hauls a long train of open wagons from the exchange sidings to the yard at Shepherdswell in August 1937. This locomotive was purchased from the Southern Railway in June 1935 at a cost of £850 to the company, replacing O class 0-6-0 tender goods No. 8, which, together with No. 1, the Fox Walker 0-6-0 saddle tank, were later sold to Cohen's scrap dealers for £95. It's a mystery why this locomotive was numbered 100; it was later renumbered No. 2 in November 1945, after an overhaul and repaint. *(Ivor Gotheridge Collection)*

The East Kent Railway stop board, on the section of line from the main line exchange sidings to Shepherdswell station on 17 February 1951.
(Dennis Cullum/ Lens of Sutton Association)

The opposite side of the stop board, looking back towards the main line exchange sidings; note the home signal controlling movement towards the main line and the long siding to the right, full of stored open wagons, August 1937. *(J.W. Sparrow Collection)*

A rare picture of Kerr Stuart constructed Victory class 0-6-0 tank No. 4 in use hauling a train, from the exchange sidings to Shepherdswell yard c1921, shortly after arriving on the EKR. The locomotive was one of a class of ten machines, constructed by Kerr Stuart for the Railway Operations Department British Army, where it was meant to be No. 602; however, it was one of the batch to be transferred to the Inland Waterways and Docks Department, as their No. 11, being sent to Richborough Port. The locomotive was purchased for £3,438 and initially owned jointly by the East Kent Colliery Company and the Guilford & Waldershare Colliery Company, both companies having a hire purchase agreement. The locomotive did not become EKR No. 4 for some time, as there was a legal dispute over traffic rates and debts from the concession period, which was not resolved until 1932, after which it became No. 4 on the EKR books. *(Ivor Gotheridge Collection)*

Ex-Weston Clevedon & Portishead 0-6-0 saddle tank Walton Park, EKR No. 2, simmers by the water column at Shepherdswell Yard, c1935. This picture looks towards Eythorne, with the high embankment in the background which had a long siding running along the top. *(Author's Collection)*

EKR No. 2 *Walton Park* at Shepherdswell locomotive shed and works on 18 July 1936, while undergoing a heavy overhaul. The shed building is in a rundown condition, with most of the far wall missing, while locomotives 4 and 6 can be seen in the picture. *(Photomatic)*

Shepherdswell shed a few months earlier on 2 May 1936, with 01 class 0-6-0 tender goods No. 100, outside the shed and locomotives 4 and 6 inside the building. Locomotive No. 2 is still undergoing a long heavy overhaul, on the far left, with most of its fittings missing, including the boiler and saddle tank. *(S.W. Baker)*

A general view of the shed and yard taken in the late 1920s, showing the trackwork and the sidings occupied with old Ex-SE&CR four wheeled carriages and a single Southern Railway eight-plank open wagon, at the head of the line. The locomotives are No. 8 Ex-SE&CR, O class, 0-6-0 tender goods and Victory class 0-6-0 tank No. 4 in the foreground with Ex-L&SWR Adams Radial tank No. 5, outside the locomotive shed, in the far distance. *(Author's Collection)*

A later view of the rebuilt locomotive shed, on 2 September 1938, showing the approach trackwork from the Eythorne end of the line. The approach sidings are full of internal user open wagons of various origins and steam drifts from a locomotive on shed in the far distance.
(R.S. Carpenter Collection)

A clear view of the trackwork at the shed, showing the points and sidings fanning out from the Eythorne end of the yard, c1938. There seems to be less clutter in this picture, with fewer derelict carriages and wagons on view. In the distance, an O1 class simmers at the approach to Shepherdswell station and stock waits in the station to form the next train to Canterbury Road. *(Ivor Gotheridge Collection)*

Locomotives No. 4 and No. 5 stand on a storage road near the water tanks, at the shed, c1930; the watering facilities seem to be a rather basic arrangement, with iron tanks supported by bulks of timber, in a long row. *(Ivor Gotheridge Collection)*

Kerr Stuart constructed Victory class 0-6-0 tank No. 4, is undergoing a heavy overhaul on 17 June 1939, with its wheels removed and jacked up on bulks of timber. This locomotive was painted in lined light olive green at this time, in a style not unlike the later Maunsell Southern Railway livery, with yellow straw lettering and lining. *(R.F. Roberts, Stephenson Locomotive Society)*

Ex-L&SWR Adams Radial tank No. 5 at Shepherdswell on 29 July 1939 during a rare period of use on the line. *(S.W. Baker)*

No. 6 storms up the bank out of Golgotha tunnel, towards Shepherdswell, with a coal train from Tilmanstone colliery, c1938. This locomotive had a long career on the East Kent Railway, being purchased in May 1923 for £800. This proved to be a very good investment as the locomotive remained in traffic right through to nationalisation in 1948 and remained in traffic until passenger services ceased in October of that year, when it was finally withdrawn. *(Ivor Gotheridge Collection)*

The approach to Golgotha tunnel, from the Eastern end, c1913, showing the freshly cut chalk cutting and the portal for a double track line, which was never constructed. The alignment on the right of the picture had large blocks of uncut chalk right through the formation of the tunnel, being bricked along the ceiling and rough cut in chalk along the sides. *(Ivor Gotheridge Collection)*

Inside Golgotha tunnel looking towards Eythorne on 17 February 1951, giving a view from the track bed, with the confines of the tunnel and the chalk cutting beyond. *(Dennis Cullum, Lens of Sutton Association)*

The junction at Eythorne, looking back towards Guilford Colliery, on 3 March 1951; this picture shows the track arrangement, for the station goods yard and the loop, with the derelict Guilford Colliery branch running off to the far left. *(Dennis Cullum, Lens of Sutton Association)*

Early construction at the Guilford (Waldershare) Colliery, c1911, showing the construction of the colliery buildings. Lack of adequate transport for materials dogged this project in its early stages, with the company having to use local cart tracks and lanes to bring in the necessary materials by horse and cart. The railway branch to this site was not constructed until 1912, after which things much improved for the ongoing work required to finish the surface buildings and sink the shafts. *(Author's Collection)*

Guilford Colliery, c1912, showing the rail connection and wagons of materials waiting to be unloaded for the construction of the colliery buildings and mining machinery. By this time, the pit head gear is in place and the chimney for the boiler house is already erected, ready for the main buildings to be constructed. *(Author's Collection)*

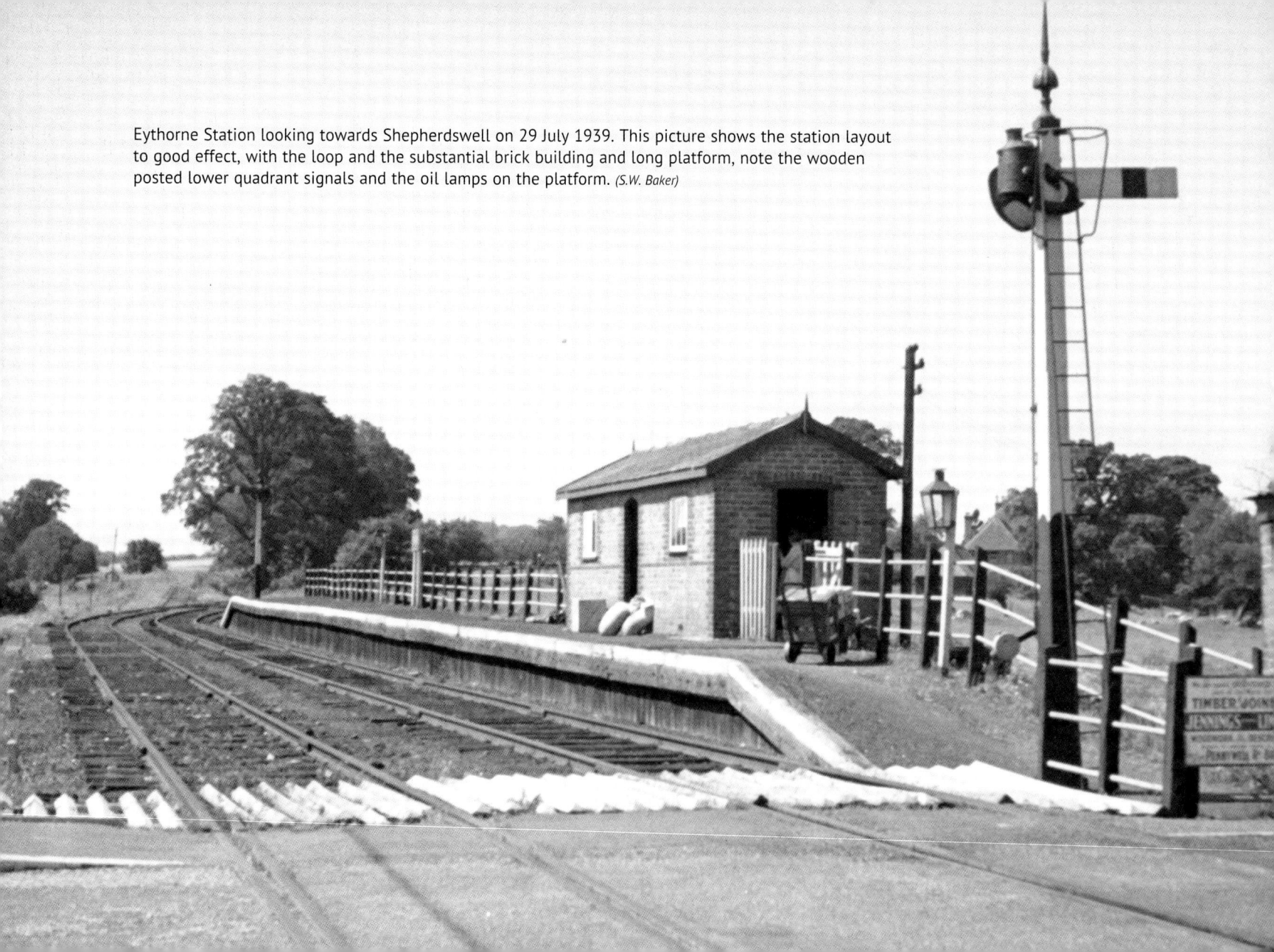

Eythorne Station looking towards Shepherdswell on 29 July 1939. This picture shows the station layout to good effect, with the loop and the substantial brick building and long platform, note the wooden posted lower quadrant signals and the oil lamps on the platform. *(S.W. Baker)*

The same location, c1958, after the closure to passengers, with the platform shortened, the fence along the back of the platform removed and the station building and hut boarded up. The goods yard and signalling have also disappeared, but the track has been relaid using bullhead rail. Through the station platform, the loop however remains in flat bottom rail. *(J.H. Aston)*

The junction for the branch to Tilmanstone Colliery pictured here on 13 March 1951, showing the signalling arrangements with lower quadrant signals and the track layout, heading off to the right towards the colliery and the main line to Canterbury Road going off into the far distance.
(Dennis Cullum, Lens of Sutton Association)

01 class 0-6-0 tender goods locomotive No. 100, heads a train of bolster and coal open wagons from Tilmanstone Colliery towards Shepherdswell in August 1937. The train is about to cross over to the main line from the colliery branch, on its way to Golgotha Tunnel.
(J.W. Sparrow Collection)

An early construction picture of Tilmanstone Colliery, c1911, showing progress on the surface buildings and the instillation of pit head gear and winding machinery. The colliery started production a year later in 1912, which coincided with the opening of the first section of the light railway. *(Author's Collection)*

Southern Railway eight-plank open wagons, loaded in the colliery yard at Tilmanstone, c1936. The large large building in the background is the washery. *(Ivor Gotheridge Collection)*

Tilmanstone Colliery from the air, showing the main buildings on the right and the washery and colliery yard on the centre left, c1935. This picture illustrates how extensive the colliery complex was during the height of coal production, with the impressive buildings around the pit head winding gear on the left and the extensive development of tracks and buildings in the centre of the picture. *(Author's Collection)*

Elvington station on 2 September 1938, showing the brick platform with its basic waiting shelter, looking towards Eastry. The station is in good condition and well kept; note the cattle grid in the foreground, a feature of most of the stations and halts on this line.
(R.S. Carpenter Collection)

Knowlton Halt looking towards Shepherdswell on 3 March 1951, with its crude timber platform edge and facing and its lack of a basic shelter or seat for any potential passenger. This was the scene two and a half years after the last passenger train, the station name board is still intact and the platform is still free from grass or any dereliction. *(Dennis Cullum, Lens of Sutton Association)*

Eastry South, c1935, showing the platform and the fenced path leading to the platform ramp from the level crossing. This picture shows the station in a well-kept condition, with newly painted fences and station name board, while the platform edge has been freshly marked in whitewash. *(Author's Collection)*

Eastry station looking towards the junction on 24 September 1938, this picture clearly shows the buildings and the two armed signal controlling the lines to Wingham and the Richborough branch. *(R.F. Roberts/ Stephenson Locomotive Society)*

A general view of Eastry station, on 15 September 1936 showing the platform, timber building and run around loop, with its heavy poundage track, note the catch point on the middle right. This picture also shows the signalling arrangements for the line to Shepherdswell in the far distance. *(J.H.L. Adams)*

Eastry station from the other direction, looking towards the junction. This picture shows the double armed signal controlling the lines to Richborough Port, far right and the line to Canterbury road far left. The grounded van body and signal ground frame shed are of interest; by this time, British Railways had taken over and removed the point nearest the road overbridge, thus making the former loop a siding, 13 March 1951. *(Lens of Sutton Collection)*

A further view of Eastry taken from the platform, c1936, looking towards the junction, clearly showing the double arm signal and a pump trolley by the grounded van body. *(Author's Collection)*

Locomotive No. 2, formally *Walton Park*, passes over the road bridge with a passenger train, c1938. *(Author's Collection)*

The junction with the line to Richborough Port in the centre and the formation on the embankment to the left heading towards Canterbury Road, 24 September 1938. *(R.S. Carpenter)*

A second picture of the overbridge at Eastry station, showing the narrow road running off into the distance, 2 September 1938. *(R.F. Roberts/Stephenson Locomotive Society)*

Woodnesborough station, c1936, showing the platform, timber building and steel four rail fence at one end and the two rail timber fence at the other. The station has recently been painted and tidied up in this pre-war picture, probably to try and win back some passengers from the local buses. *(Author's Collection)*

Ash Town station looking towards Canterbury Road, on 2 September 1938, showing the small timber shelter and the combination of steel rail fence and in the far distance, the two-rail timber fence. *(R.S. Carpenter Collection)*

An overall view of Staple station, with its brick building and wind pump for the water tower taken in August 1937. This station had a considerable amount of agricultural traffic, which included vegetables, fruit and cut flowers. The large corrugated iron building behind the station platform, was used by C.W. Darley Ltd, wholesale vegetable merchants. Note the grounded body of carriage No. 3, a former Cheshire Lines Committee vehicle, now used as an office. During the Second World War, this station handled ammunition for a nearby RAF station, which added to the much needed traffic on the line. *(R.S. Carpenter Collection)*

Staple station looking towards Shepherdswell, showing the goods platform on the right and the main station platform on the left, 2 September 1938. *(R.S. Carpenter)*

The water tower at Staple, looking towards Shepherdswell. This is a makeshift affair with bulks of timber as its legs and two large industrial water tanks providing water storage, 14 October 1950. *(D. Cullum, Lens of Sutton Association)*

Another view of Staple station showing the building and watering arrangements, c1938.
(C.F. Clapper, Copyright The Bus Archive)

01 class No. 6 waits at Staple station on 25 April 1947, with a mixed train for Wingham Canterbury Road, the introduction of the two ex-L&SWR bogie corridor carriages, Nos. 5 and 6, much improved the comfort for passengers on the line. *(Photomatic)*

Wingham Colliery Halt, on 14 October 1950, looking bleak and uninviting in this autumn picture. This halt would have served the nearby colliery, if it had opened in the early 1920s. The colliery surface buildings were constructed and later used by an engineering company specialising in the repair of agricultural machinery. *(Lens of Sutton Association)*

Ilfracombe goods locomotive East Kent Railway No. 3, stands in the platform at Wingham Town station, with a train for Shepherdswell, c1923. Unlike the Ilfracombe goods locomotives on the other Colonel Stephens lines, No. 3 was in original Beattie condition, as constructed by Beyer Peacock in 1880, although it did possess a later design of tender, the class originally having small, square-looking four wheeled tenders. No. 3 appeared on the line in 1918 when it was purchased by the company, for use on passenger and mixed train services. This is wonderful period picture with the local lady with her baby and pram and the locomotive crew attending to their elderly locomotive; the carriage is an ex-Midland vehicle. *(Author's Collection)*

Wingham Town station shortly after a repaint, c1927, with Walton Park No. 2 at the head of a single Ex-L&SWR six wheeler brake carriage, No. 5. This picture shows the track layout to good effect and the timber constructed station building, with its garden shed look, note the platform furniture, the rather basic bench and the oil lamps along the platform. *(Local Commercial Postcard)*

A later picture of Wingham Town, with a different design of timber building on the platform. Also, the oil lamps are now gone, but the wooden bench seat still beckons, 2 September 1938. *(R.S. Carpenter Collection)*

Locomotive No. 2, formerly *Walton Park*, makes black smoke, while waiting to leave the siding at Canterbury Road, in June 1939. This siding was used to reverse trains that arrived at Canterbury Road from Shepherdswell, this being done by gravity, the train crew uncoupling the carriage from the locomotive and allowing the carriage, complete with any passengers, to run down a slope in the track into the siding, the guard using his handbrake to stop the vehicle. Finally, to cap it all, the passengers got out of the carriage by using a porter's barrow as a ladder, all this to avoid having to reverse the train into the platform at Canterbury Road station. The locomotive would then run into the siding to collect the carriage for the return journey, a procedure that would definitely not go down well with today's health and safety conscious world! The reason for this method of operation was that Canterbury Road station had no run round loop, and therefore this was the only way to reverse the direction of trains. *(Rev A.W. Mace/Milepost 92)*

01 class No. 100 became No. 2, after the original No. 2, formerly *Walton Park*, was sold to industry in 1943 for £575. This picture shows the new No. 2 in the siding at Canterbury Road waiting while the ex-L&SWR bogie brake number 3 is made ready to gravitate into the station platform, on 5 June 1948. *(P.J. Garland Collection)*

No. 6 simmers in the platform at Canterbury Road station, c1947, with a train for Shepherdswell consisting of a Southern Railway Maunsell van and a single bogie carriage. *(Author's Collection)*

A going-away shot, taken from the platform of Canterbury Road station, showing the level crossing and the siding on the far left, looking towards Shepherdswell, on 2 September 1938. *(R.S. Carpenter Collection)*

A detailed picture of the station at Wingham Canterbury Road, showing the platform, station building and the cutting going away to nowhere beyond. The line was meant to go on from here to Canterbury city, but petered out in a field near Wingham. This in so many ways sums up so many light railway ventures from the late nineteenth and early twentieth centuries, when motoring was not regarded as a future threat to the railway network. It became harder to find investment for minor railways after the First World War, when large numbers of cheap ex-military vehicles were disposed of by the government and returning servicemen invested their gratuity money in running road haulage and small bus companies, using them. *(Author's Collection)*

A further picture taken from the level crossing at Wingham Canterbury Road station, looking towards the station platform and the end of the line in June 1939, showing the approach to the platform and building. *(Rev A.W. Mace/ Milepost 92)*

The Richborough Port Branch

Poison Cross Halt, looking towards Richborough Port on 2 September 1938, showing the halt some years after the final passenger train ran. The infrastructure is however still looking in good shape, despite the fact that the line is now operated as a freight only line and the siding has a solitary coal wagon, so there is some traffic still. *(R.S. Carpenter Collection)*

On the same day, 2 September 1938, the photographer has reached Roman Road Halt, which again despite the lack of a passenger service, which last ran on 1 November 1928, looks in surprisingly good shape. *(R.S. Carpenter Collection)*

A forlorn looking platform and ticket hut at Sandwich Road Halt, with grass growing between the sleepers and a feel of dereliction, c1936. The block section from Poison Cross Halt to hear, had a token, with a brass plate on it, which read Poison-Sandwich. *(R.K. Blencowe Collection)*

A rare picture of a passenger train on the Richborough Port Branch, here seen at Sandwich Road Halt with O class 0-6-0 tender goods No. 8, hauling the former Kent & East Sussex Railway, first/third Brake carriage, East Kent Railway No. 1, on its way to Shepherdswell, c1926.
(Author's Collection)

The first of two bridges on the approach to Richborough Port, this bridge crossed the former SE&CR main line between Sandwich and Minster Junction, looking towards Richborough Port. *(Author's Collection)*

The second bridge which crossed the River Stour, looking towards Richborough Port, July 1937. *(R.F. Roberts/ Stephenson Locomotive Society)*

A side view of the lonely platform at Richborough Port, showing the station platform and the Pearson Dorman long siding in the foreground, that crossed the East Kent Railway, at right angles, here seen on 2 September 1938. This station was never officially opened to traffic, remaining unused from the time it was constructed until it was demolished in the early 1950s. *(R.S. Carpenter Collection)*

A track level view of Richborough Port station, looking towards Eastry, c1925, showing the bleak nature of this part of the line. You would be waiting a long time for a train here. *(Author's Collection)*

The Last Day of Passenger Traffic

The final day of passenger services, 30 October 1948, with the last train arriving at Wingham Canterbury Road station, receiving a little unwanted help from an overzealous young railway enthusiast. This was a sad occasion for both locals and those who followed light railways; however, the service had been reduced by this time to two passenger trains per day, down from the previous three. *(Author's Collection)*

On the same day, 01 Class locomotive No. 2, formally No. 100, makes ready with a single ex-L&SWR bogie corridor brake carriage, to depart for Shepherdswell, while the station agent Dick Haffrey looks out for any last passengers. *(Author's Collection)*

The British Railways Period

O1 class 0-6-0 tender goods No. 31425 runs slowly around the connecting curve at Shepherdswell on its way back to the main line after shunting the sidings at Tilmanstone Colliery, c1949. The empty yard and derelict locomotive depot can be seen in the background, also the tracks leading to the East Kent Railway passenger platform, seen on the far right. *(Author's Collection)*

The empty platform at Shepherdswell, after the station buildings were demolished, c1954, showing the platform road and the sidings in use for wagon storage. *(Rev A.W. Mace/ Milepost 92)*

01 class 31258 shunts open mineral wagons in the station approach road at Shepherdswell, on 1 June 1960. By this time, the former East Kent Railway only existed from the exchange sidings at Shepherdswell to Tilmanstone colliery, the rest of the line having been demolished from the junction for the colliery branch to both Wingham Canterbury Road and Richborough Port in the early 1950s. *(E.A. Woollard)*

Running along the cutting after leaving Golgotha tunnel, an unidentified 01 class 0-6-0 Tender goods heads a train of empty open wagons and a solitary former LMS van in this picture, c1960. *(A.W. Burgess)*

At Tilmanstone Colliery, 01 0-6-0 tender goods 31425, prepares to leave with a loaded coal train for the exchange sidings at Shepherdswell on 8 July 1959. *(J.H. Aston)*

Five years later, on 17 July 1964, 350 HP 0-6-0 diesel mechanical shunter No. D4102 runs in reverse, hauling a similar train of loaded 16-ton coal open wagons from Tilmanstone Colliery, seen in the background and Shepherdswell exchange sidings. *(R.F. Roberts/Stephenson Locomotive Society)*

350 H P 0-6-0 Diesel Mechanical shunter No. D3044 heads a train of 16-ton mineral wagons and a solitary van, at the junction of the Tilmanstone colliery branch at Eythorne in April 1960. Both classes 08 and 09 were used on the branch in British Railways days, for shunting and trip working of these colliery trains. *(Derek Cross)*

In March 1960, 01 0-6-0 tender goods 31065 heads a train of coal wagons at the same location, heading for the exchange sidings at Shepherdswell. This locomotive is now preserved on the Bluebell Railway in East Sussex, where it is one of five Ex-SE&CR locomotives resident on that line. *(Derek Cross)*

01 class 31258 crests the embankment near Tilmanstone Colliery in April 1960 while performing shunting duties, making up coal trains. *(Derek Cross)*

Contrast in motive power, a 350 H P 0-6-0 diesel mechanical shunter No. D3044 eases its train of coal wagons past the junction at Shepherdswell former East Kent Railway Station, while 01 class 0-6-0 tender goods 31065, waits in the platform with a train of open wagons for its journey to Tilmanstone Colliery in April 1960. *(Derek Cross)*

On the same day, O1 class No. 31258 rounds the curve at the junction, with a trip working to the exchange sidings at Shepherdswell. The former locomotive shed and yard has been lifted and demolished, leaving no trace of the once prominent feature, in this picture. *(Derek Cross)*

01 class No. 31258, passes through Shepherdswell main line station, with a train of mineral wagons for Dover, in April 1960. By this time, the third rail was already laid and waiting for the next phase of the Kent coast electrification, which would be the death knell for South Eastern steam traction in 1961. *(Derek Cross)*

Class 71 No. E5000 arrives at Shepherdswell exchange sidings, with a mixed freight train from Dover of ferry vans and 16-ton mineral wagons, in April 1960. The overhead catenary was installed for these electric locomotives to be able to shunt in sidings and yards, not on the third rail, these locomotives being dual overhead and third rail pick up on the 750 DC system. *(Derek Cross)*

Class 24 No. D5013 arrives at Shepherdswell with a mineral empties train and a solitary van in April 1960. Fifteen of these Sulzer Bo-Bo diesel electric locomotives were loaned to the Southern Region from 1959 to 1962 from the London Midland Region for crew training, before the Birmingham Carriage & Wagon Company Class 33 diesel electric locomotives were introduced. They were based at Hither Green in South London and Ashford, working a variety of local and main line services during their time on the South Eastern division. *(Derek Cross)*

The Weed Killing Train

1960 was probably the last time the weed killing train was steam operated on the East Kent Railway; here we see 01 Class 31065 at the junction with the main line and the branch running tender first with the train of four-wheeled and bogie stock, on its annual visit, in April 1960. *(Derek Cross)*

The train nears Tilmanstone Colliery, with its mixed collection of converted rolling stock, consisting of tank wagons, a van and old bogie stock.
(Derek Cross)

The train returns to the boarded up and derelict Eythorne station, on its journey back to the main line at Shepherdswell. *(Derek Cross)*

A final picture of the train easing around the curve at the former East Kent Railway station, on its way back to the junction with the main line at Shepherdswell. Note that, despite the imminent withdrawal of this, one of the last 01 class locomotives, Ashford works thought fit to apply a new 1956 totem to the tender during the locomotive's last overhaul. *(Derek Cross)*

Tilmanstone and Guilford Collieries

An early photograph taken during the construction of Tilmanstone colliery, c1912, with locomotive No. 1 standing in the colliery yard. In this picture, the locomotive has a makeshift rear spectacle plate to the cab made of timber and the pit head gear is well on the way to completion.
(Local Postcard)

The pithead gear at Tilmanstone Colliery, c1930, showing the original timber framed winding tower and the later more modern steel constructed winding equipment. *(Local Postcard)*

A view of the colliery taken from the road, showing the building's later pit head winding gear and the road side siding, with a Great Western five-plank open wagon and a standard LMS van awaiting use, c1938. *(R.S. Carpenter Collection)*

The junction for Tilmanstone Colliery, taken from the level crossing at Eythorne station, looking towards Elvington on 29 July 1939. *(S.W. Baker)*

The overgrown and abandoned building at Guilford Colliery on 25 February 1989. These buildings were constructed just before the outbreak of the First World War and never used for their original purpose, as the colliery never officially opened. *(J.C.V. Mitchell)*

Another view of one of the abandoned buildings at Guilford Colliery on 25 February 1989. These buildings were kept in good condition for some years after the plan to open the colliery was finally abandoned, as one can see from this picture. *(J.C.V. Mitchell)*

The Locomotive Fleet

Locomotive No. 1 at Shepherdswell shed, c1923, in its original East Kent Railway livery of either Great Western Brunswick green, or plain black, with a garter crest, displaying its number in the centre. This locomotive was constructed by Fox Walker of Bristol 1875 and originally belonged to the Whitland & Cardigan Railway, which was taken over by the Great Western Railway in 1890, when this locomotive became No. 1386. It was sold to the Bute Works Supply Company in September 1911 and was quickly sold on to the East Kent Railway, where it became their No. 1. It originally had an open backed cab, later reconstructed with this neat steel spectacle plate, as seen here. No. 1 hauled the first official trains on the East Kent Railway, the first official freight train in October 1911 and the shareholders' special in November 1912, when it hauled the former Kent & East Sussex Railway bogie brake carriage. *(Author's Collection)*

No. 1 again during its early years on the railway, here seen running light at Eastry station, c1920, still in largely good condition and well maintained at this time. The locomotive had been reconstructed at Swindon Works by the Great Western in 1887, during the period that the Cardigan & Whitland Railway was being worked by the Great Western, before full purchase of that company. *(Stephenson Locomotive Society)*

No. 1 in store at Shepherdswell, c1930, the directors later decided to dispose of No. 1, along with 0 class 0-6-0 tender goods No. 8 in 1935, both being sold to George Cohen & Sons for £95. *(Author's Collection)*

Locomotive No. 2, *Walton Park*, was originally supplied to the Weston Clevedon & Portishead Light Railway in Somerset, by Hudswell Clarke of Leeds in May 1908, at the cost of £1,200. *Walton Park*, named after a wayside halt on the Weston Clevedon & Portishead Railway, after a short period was found to be damaging the lightly laid, flat bottomed rail of the light railway. As a result of this, Colonel Stephens had the locomotive transferred to firstly the Shropshire & Montgomeryshire Light Railway, where again it was found to be wanting at its new home, possibly because the track on the Shropshire & Montgomeryshire was also of quite light rail, hence the sale of the two almost new Hawthorn Leslie 0-6-2 tanks to the War Department, because they damaged the track. *Walton Park* was yet again transferred to a new home, this time to the East Kent Railway in April 1913, which had heavy duty flat bottomed rail, where it was successfully used in traffic, here seen at Shepherdswell, 7 July 1923. *(A.W. Croughton)*

No. 2 *Walton Park*, in store at Shepherdswell locomotive shed in the late 1920s, awaiting an overhaul. *(Author's Collection)*

No. 2 *Walton Park* from the smokebox end, in store at Shepherdswell shed, c1935. *(Author's Collection)*

No. 2 after the removal of its nameplates and repainting into Maunsell lined light olive green. No. 2 was later sold to T.W. Ward & Company in November 1943, for £575, here seen at Shepherdswell on 17 June 1939. The locomotive saw further industrial service at the Purfleet Deep Water Wharf & Storage Company in Essex, where it was named *Churchill*, being sold for scrap in 1957. *(R.F. Roberts/ Stephenson Locomotive Society)*

No. 3 was an ex-London & South Western Railway Ilfracombe 0-6-0 tender goods locomotive No. 394, here seen at Shepherdswell shed, shortly after delivery to the East Kent Railway in November 1918. At first, this locomotive was rented by the company for £200 per annum, being finally purchased in 1926. The locomotive remained in its Holly Green L&SWR livery for a long time, perhaps indicating that the agreement with the L&SWR and later the Southern Railway, could be curtailed and the locomotive returned to its owner. It is here seen taking water at Shepherdswell, 23 January 1919. *(Ken Nunn/Ivor Gotheridge Collection)*

On the same day, 394 simmers at the cold bleak platform at Shepherdswell station, with a train of four- and six-wheeler carriages, awaiting the road with a passenger service. *(Ken Nunn/Ivor Gotheridge Collection)*

After purchase in 1926, 394 became East Kent Railway No. 3, giving a few more years' service on passenger and light freight trains. It was eventually withdrawn from service in 1927 and left to rust in peace at the end of a siding at Shepherdswell, until finally sold for scrap for £60 in 1934; so ended the life of the last original Beattie, Bayer Peacock Ilfracombe goods locomotive. *(Author's Collection)*

A works photograph of the East Kent Railways locomotive that never was, the original No. 4, Gabrielle, here seen in photographic works grey. This was one of two locomotives ordered from R.W. Hawthorn Leslie & Co of Newcastle upon Tyne, shortly before the outbreak of the First World War; however the company found that its funds could not stretch to purchasing them, so they were both sold to other customers. The first locomotive seen here was sold to the Wemyss Coal Company in May 1914, being delivered to Wellesley Colliery near Methil in Fife, as their No. 15, remaining there until 1972, when it was scrapped. The second locomotive was to be named *Rowena*; it was delivered to Sir John Jackson Ltd at Porton Camp Wiltshire in November 1914, it's a bit obscure if it was War Department or contractor's property. However, it was later transferred to the Kinmel Park Camp Military Railway, near Rhyl in North Wales, being named Northumbria and numbered WD1. After the war, this locomotive was sold to the Ebbw Vale steelworks, becoming their No. 36. Later, in 1936, it was transferred to Redburn Iron & Steel Company and gave many years good service, being scrapped in 1963. *(Author's Collection)*

The locomotive that became No. 4, a Kerr Stuart Victory Class 0-6-0 tank, one of ten constructed in 1917 for the War Department, where it was allocated No. 602, in the ROD list. However, before this could happen the locomotive was transferred to the IWDD, operating at Richborough Military Port, which was an extensive War Department port facility during the First World War, for supplying the British army in France and the Western Front. In 1919, the whole class was sold off by the government war disposals board and 602, IWDD11, became the property of the Guilford Colliery Company, later being transferred to the East Kent Railway Company, becoming No. 4. Recorded here in its original lined IWDD grey livery at Shepherdswell shed, c1920, this workmanlike heavy shunting locomotive was a very welcome addition to the railway's largely elderly second- and third-hand fleet of locomotives. *(Ken Nunn/Ivor Gotheridge Collection)*

Dumped at the ash pit, No. 4 stands awaiting its next turn of heavy shunting and trip working from Tilmanstone Colliery on 29 May 1930, here seen at Shepherdswell locomotive shed. *(S.W. Baker)*

No. 4 in its later condition, painted in lined Maunsell light olive green, with the later pattern smoke box door, c1938.
(Author's Collection)

A further picture of No. 4 in its later guise, with the shed water crane in the foreground. This is a good view of the locomotive, showing the later olive green livery and style of plain yellow lettering, c1939. *(Author's Collection)*

The opposite side of the locomotive, showing the features in detail. No. 4 stayed in traffic until nationalisation in 1948, when it was allocated a British Railways number 30948, but never carried it, being cut up at Ashford Works in 1949. *(Photomatic)*

Locomotive No. 5 was an unusual choice for motive power on a light railway, in that it was designed to haul fast trains out of Waterloo to the south-western suburbs. Constructed in 1885 by Neilson of Glasgow, becoming London & South Western Railway No. 488, it spent the first decade of its life on suburban duties out of Waterloo. During the First World War, there was a shortage of locomotives and the Adams Radial tanks were to a large part being replaced on suburban services by other more modern tank classes and the beginnings of electrification. Later renumbered 0488, being sold in 1917 to the government for use at the Royal Naval General Salvage Depot at Ridham, near Sittingbourne, later it was moved to the General Stores Department at Belvedere. After hostilities ended, the locomotive was put up for sale along with other war surplus items, being sold to the East Kent Railway for £375, the original idea being to use the locomotive for shunting and passenger traffic on the line. However it was soon found that the 4-4-2 tank was not suitable for shunting and barely suitable for a light railway passenger service. It is here seen at Shepherdswell shed yard, c1925. *(Author's Collection)*

Two's company: 4-4-2 radial tank No. 5 in the shed yard at Shepherdswell with 0-6-0 tank No. 4, seen here c1935. No. 5 was last used on a train on the East Kent Railway on 23 May 1943, after which the locomotive was stored and later put up for sale, along with No. 2, formerly *Walton Park*, by the directors, who were only offered modest sums by two scrap dealers for No. 5. The company approached the Southern Railway for advice over a fair scrap price for the locomotive and were taken aback when the Southern purchased the locomotive as spare motive power, for use on the Lyme Regis branch, for £120. *(Author's Collection)*

No. 5 from the bunker end, showing the coal rails fitted in L&SWR days. The Adams radial tanks were probably some of the most handsome locomotives ever designed in Britain; we are very lucky that this example of the class was later sold to the Southern Railway for use on the Lyme Regis branch and survived long enough to be preserved on the Bluebell Railway in East Sussex. *(R.C. Stumpf Collection)*

An elderly driver peeps out of the cab of No. 5 in the yard of Shepherdswell in this late 1930s picture of the radial tank in its newly painted Maunsell lined light olive green livery, during a rare occasion of being in steam. *(Author's Collection)*

The Locomotive Fleet

Locomotive No. 6 was an ex-SE&CR, O class 0-6-0 tender goods, which was purchased in 1923 for £800, from the newly formed Southern Railway. No. 6 was overhauled at Ashford Works before delivery and fitted with a short chimney, of the pattern used by the ex-SER R1 class 0-6-0 tanks on the Canterbury & Whitstable Railway; this extra cost the company an additional £1 18s 11p. The purchase of No. 6 was a very good investment, in that the locomotive lasted in traffic until nationalisation in 1948, when it was finally withdrawn and scrapped. No. 6 is seen here in as delivered condition, at Shepherdswell, c1926. *(Ivor Gotheridge Collection)*

A profile view of No. 6 on the connecting line at Shepherdswell, c1925, showing the original domeless Stirling boiler, with the safety valve positioned in the centre of the boiler and the original style of lettering on the tender, with its unique combined EKR No. 6 lettering. *(Ken Nunn/ Ivor Gotheridge Collection)*

No. 6 was later reconstructed as a highbred locomotive, having features from both O and O1 classes. The reason for this cross between the two designs was to cut costs for the reconstruction, in that the locomotive had a domed H class boiler, but retained its O class Stirling round top cab and smokebox with wing plates. The reconstruction cost the company £1,500; the round top Stirling cab made No. 6 unique among the O1 class Locomotives. *(Author's collection)*

No. 6 laid up between turns at Shepherdswell shed on the 4 August 1947; behind one can just see the replacement No. 2, formerly No. 100, an O1 class. In four months, the East Kent Railway would be nationalised and taken into public ownership. No. 6 was given a new British Railways number, 31372, which it never carried, as the locomotive was cut up at Ashford Works on 25 February 1949. *(G.S. Lloyd)*

In the final year of its service, No. 6 waits in the yard at Shepherdswell for its next turn of duty, ashed and grubby but not beaten, a credit to its designer James Stirling, who produced good no-nonsense sturdy locomotives, that could do the job. This picture shows a number of features of this locomotive including the steam reverser, mounted on the running plate, halfway along the boiler, a common feature on SE&CR locomotives. *J.H. Aston)*

Locomotive No. 7 was an ex-London & South Western Railway 330 class 0-6-0 saddle tank, No. 127, constructed by Beyer Peacock in 1882. These powerful, reliable tank locomotives were a standard class of saddle tank designed by Beyer Peacock of Gorton Works Manchester, being supplied to several railways including the L&SWR and railways in Sweden; variants were also supplied to industry. E0127 was supplied second hand from the Southern Railway in 1925 for £380 and, after an overhaul at Eastleigh Works, left there in January 1926, for despatch to Shepherdswell via Rolvenden on the Kent & East Sussex Railway, where it spent several days in transit. Here it is seen at Shepherdswell not long after its arrival in 1926, in its first East Kent Railway livery of plain black with shaded EKR lettering. *(Author's collection)*

A second picture of No. 7 at Shepherdswell from the opposite side showing its fittings and general outline in May 1935. *(Ron Jarvis)*

No. 7 in steam and awaiting its next turn of duty on 29 May 1930, again at Shepherdswell, in a slightly care-worn state. This locomotive was used on passenger and freight services on the line, often seen in service on the Richborough branch, where it was a regular on the passenger service. *(S.W. Baker)*

Awaiting repairs at Shepherdswell in 1934. No. 7 required much attention by this time, which led to the locomotive receiving a new smokebox fabricated by Ashford Works on the Southern Railway, which was fitted at Shepherdswell by the East Kent Railway fitters during a long, heavy overhaul, not completed until 1936. It was also painted Maunsell light olive green and fully lined out at this time. *(Author's Collection)*

No. 7 in its later plain unlined black condition, c1938, showing its new smokebox of a different pattern to the Beyer Peacock sloped original and the Great Western patterned chimney, salvaged from the scrapped No. 1. *(Cuthbert Hamilton Ellis)*

No. 7 at Shepherdswell, c1939. The Southern Railway later bid for the locomotive, offering £90 for it and it was cut up at Ashford Works on 23 of March 1946; only the whistle is reputed to still exist, rescued by one of the works' staff. *(Author's Collection)*

Locomotive No. 8 was an O class 0-6-0 tender goods, like No. 6, with a domeless Stirling boiler. However, the steam reverser was in the cab and not fitted to the running plate. No. 8 was acquired from the Southern Railway for £1,085, arriving on the East Kent Railway on 22 September 1928. Like No. 6. it originally had a Whitstable short chimney; unlike No. 6, the locomotive had a short career on the East Kent Railway, being withdrawn and sold for scrap in 1935. Here, No. 8 waits in the yard at Shepherdswell, for its next turn of duty, c1930, while a plume of grey smoke drifts from its chimney. *(Author's Collection)*

No. 8 arrives at the approach to Shepherdswell East Kent Station, with a train of two elderly four-wheeled carriages, Nos. 8 and 9, both former London Chatham & Dover Railway vehicles, c1930. Note the line of wagons in the background with No. 5, the ex-L&SWR Adams Radial 4-4-2 tank in store. *(Author's Collection)*

In the afternoon shadows, No. 8 waits on the siding at Canterbury Road with a return train for Shepherdswell, c1932, consisting of the former Kent & East Sussex Railway bogie brake. Three wagons are awaiting loading at the end of the siding, while the locomotive crew attend to the locomotive for the return journey. *(Author's Collection)*

No. 8 towards the end of its working life, on 22 April 1935, in a rundown leaky condition, with steam oozing out from various parts of the locomotive and patchwork repairs to the smokebox door. No. 8 was withdrawn and cut up for scrap during 1935, being sold for £95.
(R.C. Stump Collection)

A locomotive with an optimistic number, East Kent Railway No. 100 seen here in the siding at Canterbury Road, with a passenger service for Shepherdswell, consisting of a single London Chatham & Dover Railway six-wheeled brake carriage, No. 10, c1938. No. 100 started life as an O class 0-6-0 tender goods No. 383, being constructed by Sharp Stuart of Glasgow for the South Eastern Railway in 1893; it was reconstructed to an O1 class in 1908. With the withdrawal of No. 8, there was a need to replace the locomotive in the East Kent Railway fleet, so the company approached the Southern Railway for a replacement and were offered 1383 in exchange for No. 8 and the tender from No. 6, after the tender from No. 8 was exchanged with No. 6. The Southern Railway sold No. 1383 to the East Kent Railway for £850 in 1935, as a replacement locomotive. *(Rev A.W.V Mace, Milepost 92)*

No one can quite work out why No. 100 acquired that number. It might have been a mistake made at Ashford Works in 1935, or some have said that there was an attempt to renumber all the locomotives on all the Colonel Stephens railways and No. 100 was the first renumbered and the last – we will now probably never know. However, nothing is forever and in time No. 100 was renumbered 2 to replace the old No. 2, *Walton Park*. This was done in November 1945, when the locomotive was being overhauled at Ashford Works. No. 2 is seen here at Shepherdswell yard in 1948, shortly after nationalisation. *(J.H. Aston)*

No. 2 from the other side seen while shunting at Shepherdswell on 12 June 1947. By this time the attractive lined Maunsell light olive green livery had given way to plain unlined black. *(F. Butterfield)*

Awaiting the road at Shepherdswell East Kent Railway station on the 5 June 1948, this is a good picture of No. 2 from the tender, looking down the side of the locomotive. No. 2 was transferred to Dover shed in 1948, when the shed at Shepherdswell closed. It was overhauled in 1949 at Ashford Works, becoming British Railways 31383, withdrawn 7 April 1950 and scrapped on 24 April 1951. By this time, the older rolling stock had been cleared from the railway and the passenger stock consisted of two more modern ex-L&SWR bogie corridor brake vehicles, acquired from the Southern Railway. *(P.J. Garland)*

1371 was the final locomotive acquired by the railway; arriving in March 1944, it was purchased from the Southern Railway for £1,125 and was never repainted in East Kent Railway livery or given a new number. This locomotive continued to operate in Southern Railway livery, with Bulleid sunshine lettering numbers until taken into British Railways stock in 1948. It started life as South Eastern Railway 0 class 0-6-0 tender goods No. 371, constructed by Sharp Stuart of Glasgow in 1891 and reconstructed as an 01 class in 1909. It became Southern Railway A371 in 1923 and 1371 in 1931, having at first a lined black livery and later a plain unlined black livery. Its main claim to fame is that it was one of the locomotives used to pilot trains during the Dunkirk evacuations, when it assisted trains up Hildenborough bank. After nationalisation in 1948, it was allocated a British Railways number, 31371, but this was never applied and 1371 was withdrawn on the 8 January 1949. *(J.H. Aston)*

01 0-6-0 tender goods 1381 in store at Shepherdswell locomotive shed, c1947, between running turns, on hire to the East Kent Railway from the Southern Railway, who were often called on for extra motive power, when there was ether a locomotive shortage due to overhauls or repairs taking place to the company's fleet of locomotives. *(Author's Collection)*

Locomotives on Loan to the East Kent Railway

Rother Valley, later Kent & East Sussex Railway No. 2, *Northiam*, here seen at Shepherdswell shed while on hire to the East Kent Railway in 1923. This locomotive had an interesting career in the world of light railways, in that it hauled the first train on the Rother Valley Railway from Robertsbridge to Tenterden (Rolvenden) on 2 April 1900. One of two identical locomotives constructed by Hawthorn Leslie in 1899, for the Rother Valley Railway, the other locomotive, No. 1, was named *Tenterden*. It spent time away from its home railway on the Weston Clevedon & Portishead Railway in 1919 and had several spells on hire to the East Kent Railway, firstly in 1913, when it was used as a contractor's locomotive and in 1923, when it returned to the line. Perhaps its finest hour being during the making of the Will Hay film *Oh, Mr Porter!* when it was used by Gainsborough Pictures, on the recently closed Basingstoke & Alton Light Railway, where it was named *Gladstone*. No. 2 *Northiam* was withdrawn and later scrapped in 1941 at Rolvenden, on the Kent & East Sussex Railway. *(Author's Collection)*

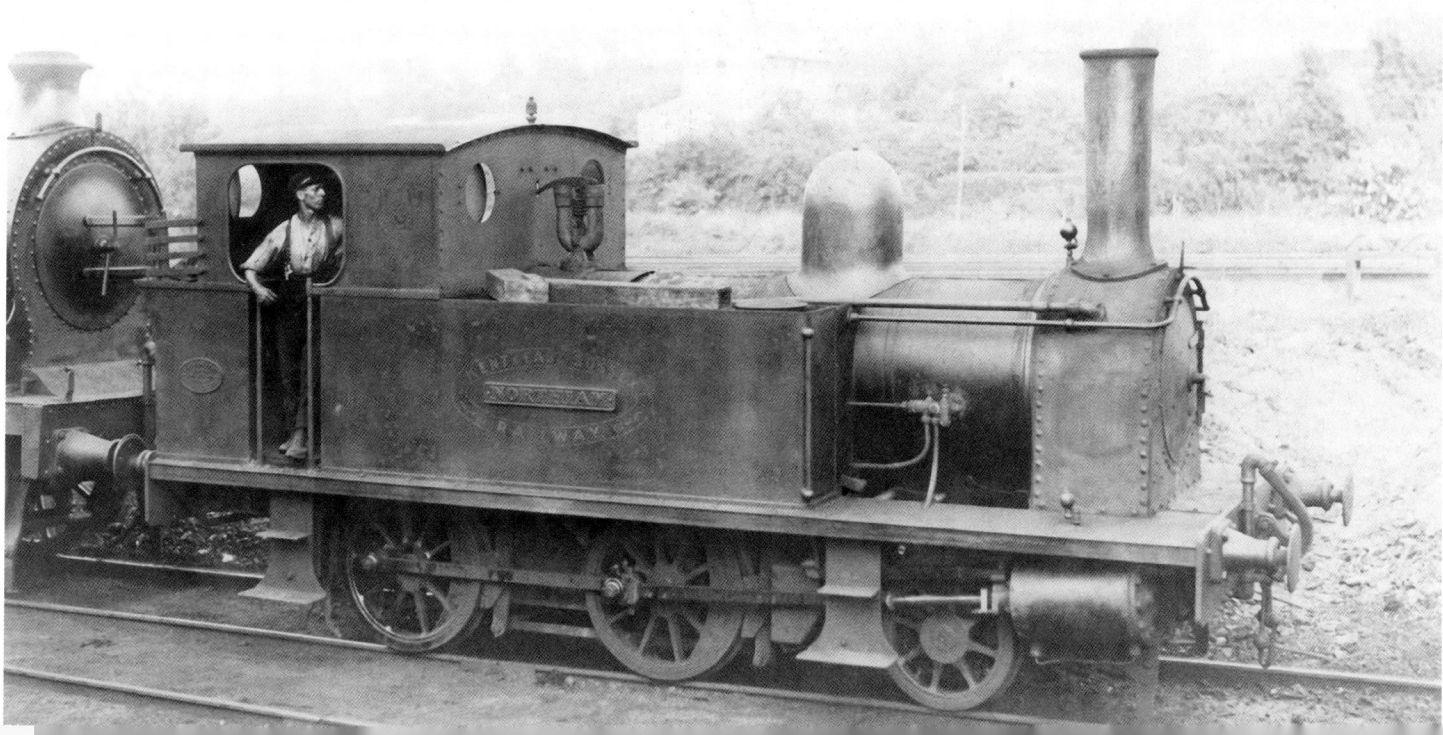

Northiam again at Shepherdswell shed on 28 September 1929, during a further period of hiring from the Kent & East Sussex Railway. *Northiam* had a livery of Oxford blue with vermillion lining, which included the company's title in an oval garter encircling the nameplate. As the years went by, the blue livery became more careworn until the locomotive looked matt black under the layers of grime. *(H.F. Wheeler)*

Northiam in company with ex-L&SWR Adams Radial No. 5 at Shepherdswell shed on 14 September 1923, during a period between operating turns on the line. *(Ken Nunn/Ivor Gotheridge Collection)*

Another Kent & East Sussex locomotive that spent periods on hire to the East Kent Railway was No. 4, *Hecate*, the 0-8-0 tank. This locomotive was constructed in 1904 by Hawthorn Leslie of Newcastle for use on heavy trains up Tenterden Bank and possibly for the planned extension to Maidstone, which never happened. The 0-8-0 tank would see only limited use on the Kent & East Sussex Railway, being steamed once a week to keep it in working order and only used on the Rolvenden to Headcorn section, owing to its weight. *Hecate* was hired to the East Kent Railway during the First World War, when it was used on heavy coal trains from Tilmanstone colliery to the exchange sidings at Shepherdswell, being returned in 1922 to its home railway. After Colonel Stephens died in 1931, W.H. Austin arranged with the Southern Railway to take *Hecate* in exchange for ex-L&SWR E0330 class saddle tank No. 0335 and two spare boilers. 0335 became the new No. 4 on the Kent & East Sussex Railway and *Hecate* became Southern Railway No. 949, being allocated the number 30949 and withdrawn in 1950 by British Railways. *(Author's Collection)*

The Carriage Stock

Carriage No. 1 was an ex-Kent & East Sussex Railway, R.Y. Pickering constructed bogie vehicle, delivered as part of a three carriage set in May 1905. The other two vehicles were later sold to the War Department and served on a number of military railways; however, the carriage that was to become East Kent Railway No. 1, was transferred to the line in 1912 and used from the opening until the line was nationalised in 1948. Here it is seen in store at Shepherdswell in the late 1930s; it was originally painted dark brown and ivory white, later repainted dark red and finally a medium grey colour. *(G.A. Hookham)*

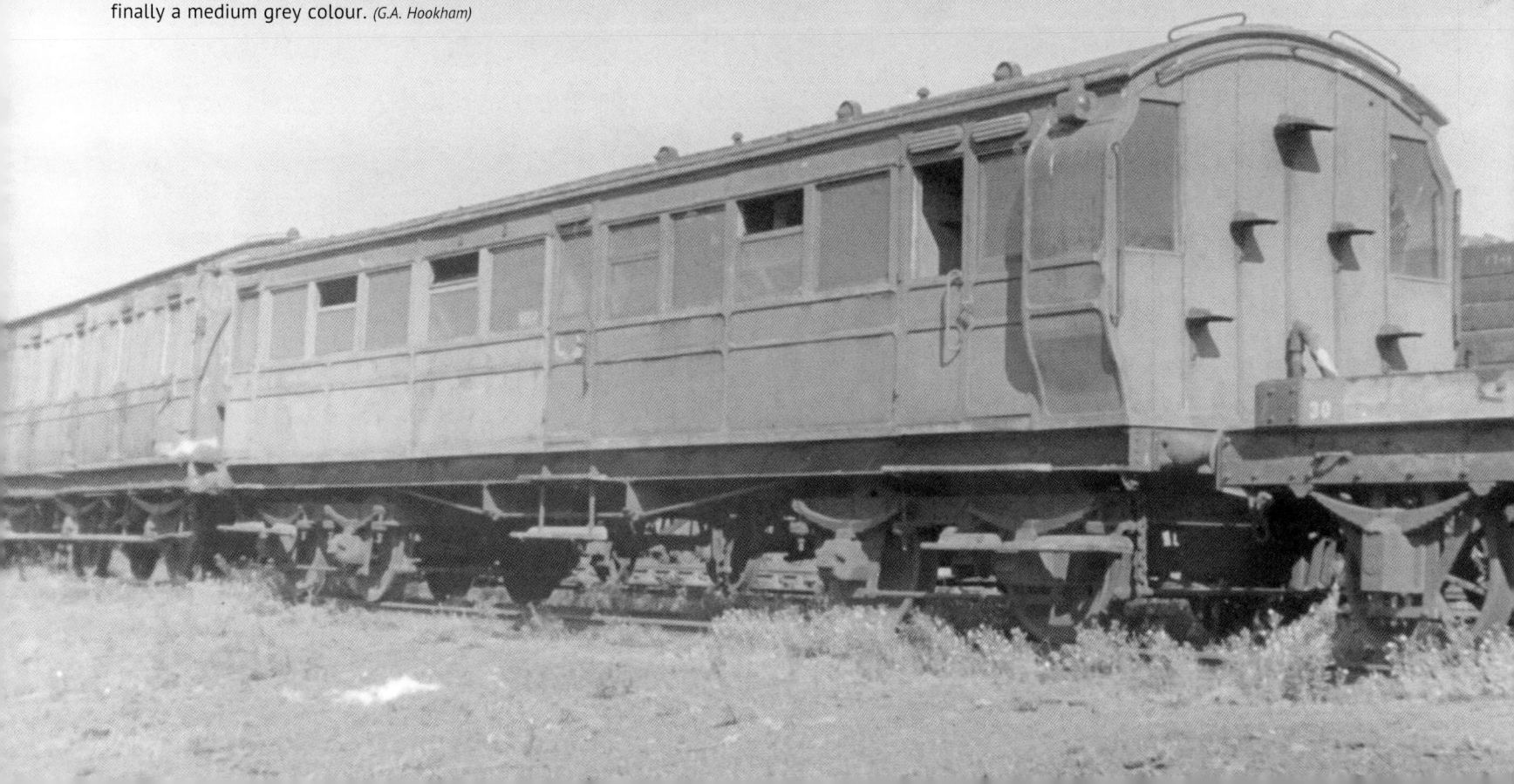

Carriage No. 1 shunted to the back of the station platform at Shepherdswell, showing signs of neglect, with ivory white paint coming through the layers of dark red in this late 1930s picture. *(Author's Collection)*

Carriage No. 2 is seen here being patched up towards the end of its long life, here seen in the yard at Shepherdswell, painted in light grey livery, c1946. *(Author's Collection)*

Carriage No. 2 was an ex-North London Railway passenger brake van, originally purchased for use on the Kent & East Sussex Railway, where it was one of two, being transferred to the East Kent Railway in 1913 and much used in the early days after the line opened. It was originally painted dark brown and ivory white, but was later painted light grey, surviving until around 1946, when it was broken up. *(Rev A.W.V. Mace, Milepost 92)*

Carriage No. 3 was an ex-Cheshire Lines Committee four-wheeler first third vehicle, constructed at Gorton Works Manchester, by the Manchester Sheffield and Lincolnshire Railway in 1870, here seen painted grey, among a line of derelict carriage stock, on 24 September 1938. This carriage was one of two four-wheeled vehicles purchased in 1902 for use on the Kent & East Sussex Railway, becoming their No. 12. It was transferred to the East Kent Railway in 1913, being used on workmen's trains, later being stored for some years in the carriage siding at Shepherdswell, after which its body was sold in 1946 to become a summer house. *(R.F. Roberts, Stephenson Locomotive Society)*

Carriage No. 4 was an ex-Midland Railway six-wheel first, third compartment vehicle constructed at Derby in 1882. Originally a slip carriage on the Midland Railway, it was purchased for £180 by Colonel Stephens 1919 for use on the East Kent Railway, surviving until 1948, when it was scrapped. *(Photomatic)*

Carriage No. 5 was an ex-L&SWR six-wheeled brake third vehicle, thought to have been obtained from the War Department around 1920. This carriage gave good service and was extensively used with the Midland six-wheeler No. 4 for many years on passenger services, not being stored until the ex-L&SWR bogie carriages arrived during 1946. No. 5 was finally withdrawn and scrapped by British Railways in 1948. Here it is seen with ex-CLC four wheeler No. 3 at Shepherdswell in the late 1930s, after undergoing a repaint into dark green. *(Author's Collection)*

Carriage No. 6 was the second Cheshire Lines Committee four-wheeled vehicle, here seen in the late 1930s painted grey, in the siding at Shepherdswell. This carriage was one of a pair purchased in 1913 from the Kent & East Sussex Railway, for use on workmen's trains. It was withdrawn in 1937 and the body was removed from its chassis for use as accommodation at Staple station. *(Photomatic)*

A very derelict carriage No. 9 awaiting scrapping 25 April 1947, this former London Chatham & Dover vehicle, was obtained from the SE&CR in 1920, here seen in the dump siding at Shepherdswell, c1946. This carriage was one of three ex-LC&DR vehicles purchased in 1920 for use on workmen's trains, being withdrawn after these trains were withdrawn, finally being broken up in 1947. *(Author's Collection)*

Carriage No. 9 was part of the set of three ex-LC&DR four-wheelers purchased from the SE&CR in 1920, here seen together with No. 7, in the siding at Shepherdswell East Kent Railway station in August 1940. This vehicle was constructed as a brake third, for use on the through trains to the Great Northern Railway, using Snow Hill station and tunnel in London. It was in use until the late 1930s or up until the mid-1940s on workmen's trains, after which it was withdrawn and left derelict until broken up in March 1948. *(Rev A.W.V. Mace, Milepost 92)*

Carriage No. 10 was also an ex-LC&DR brake first, third, constructed in 1893 which was obtained from the Southern Railway in 1926 for £57 5s 9p; it still had its SE&CR number of 2663. It was later repainted Southern Railway Maunsell light olive green, being designated with two first class and one third class compartments, rather extravagant for a railway with so few first class passengers, if any passengers at all. No. 10 was in use on the line until nationalisation in 1948, when it was finally withdrawn for scrap. Here it is seen at Shepherdswell on 25 April 1947, while undergoing repairs. *(Photomatic)*

Carriage No. 11 was similar to No. 10, in that it was a former LC&DR brake third constructed in 1891, the Southern Railway charging £56 16s 8p for it. The vehicle arrived on the East Kent Railway in 1927, still carrying its SE&CR number 2691. It was later repainted in Southern Railway Maunsell light olive green, being withdrawn by British Railways in 1948 and broken up, here seen at Shepherdswell on 25 April 1947.
(Ivor Gotheridge Collection)

Towards the end of the Second World War, it was decided that the company had to replace its worn out carriage stock, an approach to the Southern Railway was made and the result being the offer of two ex-L&SWR bogie corridor brake vehicles, of the same design as those supplied to the Kent & East Sussex Railway in 1943. These carriages became Nos. 5 and 6 in the carriage fleet; both were delivered in July 1946, the brake compartment for No. 5 faced Wingham and No. 6 faced towards Shepherdswell. Both carriages operated on the line until the passenger service ceased in October 1948, when the pair were withdrawn for scrap. Carriage No. 6 is seen here at Shepherdswell on 25 April 1947; these vehicles must have been seen as the last word in luxury on this otherwise church mouse railway. *(Ivor Gotheridge Collection)*

Carriage No. 6 waits in the platform at Shepherdswell in the evening sunlight, forming part of the mixed train to Canterbury Road, c1948. At the time of delivery, the bogie carriages were numbered 3126 and 3128 in the Southern Railway list. *(Tom Middlemass Collection)*

The Wagon Fleet

A selection of second- and third-hand goods wagons used for internal traffic on the East Kent Railway, here seen dumped in the yard at Shepherdswell, c1935. These include an ex-SE&CR 6-ton open, a three-plank open and an ex-South Eastern Railway van. *(Rev A.W.V. Mace, Milepost 92)*

A former South Eastern Railway van: East Kent Railway No. 17, painted in light grey livery, with black ironwork, c1935. *(Author's Collection)*

A former South Eastern Railway four-plank open wagon No. 19, seen here at Canterbury Road siding, c1935. This elderly wagon has a number of interesting features, including early pattern self-contained buffers and Mansell wooden-centred wheels, constructed in 1864. The livery is light grey with black ironwork; these wagons were acquired at the time the line opened in 1912, for internal goods traffic.
(Author's Collection)

Ex-SER Mansell open goods wagon No. 29, here seen at Shepherdswell in 1947; this was probably one of the last wagons with Mansell carriage wheels in existence at this time. It was recorded that the East Kent Railway owned 140 wagons in 1917 but this internal fleet had sharply dwindled by 1947. *(Author's Collection)*

A pair of former SER four-plank open wagons Nos. 24 and 40, here seen on the siding at the East Kent Railway station at Shepherdswell, August 1937. Both are painted in East Kent Railway light grey, with black ironwork, No. 24 having Mansell wheels. *(J.W. Sparrow)*

On 2 September 1938, a pair of former SER open wagons stand derelict on a siding at Shepherdswell, the former SE&CR lettering working its way through the thin coat of East Kent Railway light grey paint. These wagons have cut down rounded ends. *(R.S. Carpenter Collection)*

The East Kent Railway did not use goods brake vans until the Second World War, when the company acquired a former L&SWR road van from the Southern Railway for £100, which was after negotiation reduced to £60. The van arrived in 1942 and allocated No. 34. This van remained on the railway until nationalisation, being used on mixed trains until October 1948, when passenger services ended, here seen at Shepherdswell on the 5 June 1948. Both the more modern former L&SWR bogie carriages 5–6 and this brake van were labelled for use on the East Kent section only. A second road van arrived later and the railway had a third Maunsell double veranda type brake van in 1947; however this might have been on loan from the Southern Railway. *(P.J. Garland)*

The permanent way crane, probably of Midland Railway origin, with its train of runners in store at Shepherdswell on 24 October 1931. This crane was acquired quite early on in the railway's existence and was used for engineering jobs along the line and some lifting at the works at Shepherdswell. *(Photomatic)*

The permanent way crane from the opposite side, showing the two runners, a three-plank open and an ex-LMS five-plank open, c1932.
(Author's Collection)

Shepherdswell Shed and Works

A line of East Kent Railway locomotives in the evening sun at Shepherdswell locomotive shed, showing 0-6-0 saddle tank No. 2, *Walton Park*, at the head of the line, followed by one of the ex-SE&CR 0 class locomotives, No. 6 or No. 8 and finally ex-L&SWR 0330 class 0-6-0 saddle tank No. 7 at the rear, c1930. *(Lens of Sutton Association)*

A shed full of locomotives, probably taken on a Sunday, when trains did not run on the line, with Hudswell 0-6-0 saddle tank No. 2 undergoing a heavy overhaul, O class 0-6-0 tender goods No. 6 in the shed and O1 class 0-6-0 tender goods No. 100 standing outside. Victory class 0-6-0 tank No. 4 can be seen standing inside the shed on the opposite road, 3 May 1936. *(Author's Collection)*

On the same day, a profile view, showing the No. 2 in its dismembered state and No. 100 outside the dilapidated shed. *(S.W. Baker)*

A winter scene outside in the shed yard, with No. 7, No. 6 and No. 2, in a line, c1925.
In the background can be seen the embankment and sidings, full of carriages and wagons.
(Author's Collection)

The dump siding at the rear of the locomotive shed, where withdrawn locomotives and carriages under repair were normally kept, showing the two former Cheshire Lines Committee four wheelers and an ex-London Chatham & Dover Railway four-wheel carriage dumped in the siding awaiting their fate 18 July 1936. *(Photomatic)*

A line of London Chatham & Dover Railway carriages meet there fate in the dump siding, c1947, while a line of open wagons are next in line for the breaker's hammer. *(Author's Collection)*

Cover Pictures

0 Class 0-6-0 tender goods locomotive No. 6 with train, c1925 at Shepherdswell Station. *(Author's Collection)*

Eythorne station on 2 September 1938, looking towards Shepherdswell. *(R.S. Carpenter Collection)*

The Preserved Line

Two-car class 108 DMU in the platform at Shepherdswell, c1995. The Network Southeast livery would have been familiar to visitors as it was worn by the trains serving the neighbouring main line station at the time this picture was taken. *(Graeme Gleaves)*

Looking very out of place is the class 107 DMU. The second vehicle behind it to the left of the picture is the experimental Leyland coach.
(Graeme Gleaves)

Pictured in September 2019 under restoration is long-term resident English Electric 0-6-0 diesel locomotive *Richborough Castle*. *(Graeme Gleaves)*

Eythorne station, April 2018. The newly delivered class 457 car sits in the bay platform and a class 08 waits in the main platform waiting to return to Shepherdswell. *(Graeme Gleaves)*

The view looking back up the line from Eythorne station, October 2019. The hut that houses the station ground frame is on the right and visible against the line of trees on the left is the cleared formation of the Guilford Colliery line. *(Graeme Gleaves)*

Class 08, No. 08799 with a train comprised of a pair of BR Mk. 2 coaches in the yard at Shepherdswell. *(Matthew Plews)*

The 4-VEP driving trailer composite at Shepherdswell on 25 September 2019. The railway is the only location you can currently ride in an example of this class of train at present. *(Graeme Gleaves)*

Peckett 0-4-0 saddle tank *Achilles* pictured at Eythorne in September 2019 having just arrived with a service from Shepherdswell.